Getting Up

Detail from a Seen One whole car.
Henry Chalfant

The MIT Press
Cambridge, Massachusetts
London, England

Getting Up

Subway Graffiti in New York

Craig Castleman

This book was set in Compu-
graphic ITC Bookman by
County Photo Compositing
Corp., and printed and bound
in the United States of America.

Library of Congress Cataloging
in Publication Data

Castleman, Craig.
    Getting up.

    Bibliography: p.
    1. Graffiti—New York (N.Y.)
2. New York (N.Y.)—Social life
and customs. I. Title.
GT3913.N72C37   1982
302.2'244   82-8957
ISBN 0-262-03089-6 (hard)   AACR2
    0-262-53051-1 (paper)
ISBN-13 978-0-262-03089-2 (hard)
        978-0-262-53051-4 (paper)

20 19 18 17 16 15 14

With love to my parents, Midge and Ed Castleman

Contents

Preface

New York City teenagers have been "getting up"—marking and painting their names on subway trains—since the late 1960s. Beginning with the simple attempts of a few early writers, the movement has grown to involve thousands of young people whose name writing now frequently amounts to the painting of enormous and colorful murals.

Since 1971 the New York City government and the Metropolitan Transportation Authority (MTA), the state authority that operates the city's subways, have devoted tremendous amounts of energy and money to efforts to eradicate graffiti. Most estimates put these city and state expenditures at more than $150 million. Unfortunately, there has been very little press coverage of or public interest in the cost or effectiveness of the city's and the MTA's antigraffiti programs. Nor has much effort been made to examine the nature of the graffiti-writing phenomenon itself.

The purpose of this study is to introduce the reader to graffiti writers and graffiti writing and to outline the history of the city government's and the MTA's efforts to eliminate what former city council president Sanford Garelik called "one of the worst forms of pollution we have to combat." Throughout its preparation I have taken as a guidepost the suggestion made by my academic advisers at Columbia University, Margaret Mead and Louis Forsdale, that this be a strictly descriptive study, not an analysis of the overall meaning or social significance of graffiti writing. I especially valued Professor Forsdale's suggestion that "this isn't the time to worry about *why* people write and fight graffiti, because we aren't sure yet just what it is that they are doing. Find that out first. People can argue about what it all means later on."

Most of the information in this book is derived from tape-recorded personal interviews with graffiti writers, transit police officers, active and former public officials, MTA employees, and other interested parties. Chapter 1 consists solely of a verbatim transcription of a portion of an interview with a graffiti writer named Lee.

Although interviewing constituted the bulk of my field research, I also used newspaper and magazine clippings; reports, studies, and documents made available to me by various city agencies; and information derived from informal conversations with graffiti writers and others at subway stations, train yards, police stations, detention homes, parks, pizza shops, schools, the headquarters of graffiti organizations, and other places around New York City. Such "hanging out" was not only informative; it was a pleasure.

A few terms are used with which readers may not be familiar. Although most of them are defined in the text, there are two that might best be defined at the outset.

Writers. New York's graffiti writers have been referred to as "graffitists," "artists," "scrawlers," "daubers," "vandals," "insecure cowards," and a variety of other names. They generally refer to themselves, however, as "writers," and that is the name I use.

Graffiti. The word *graffiti* (from the Italian *graffiare*, "to scratch") has been used to describe many different sorts of wall writings including prehistoric cave paintings, "latrinalia" (bathroom-wall writings), and a wide variety of political, sexual, humorous, and self-identifying messages that have been scratched, painted, and marked on walls throughout history. The term will do as well to describe the train paintings of New York's subway writers. In common usage, graffiti is used as a singular noun, and I do so as well.

Acknowledgments

Special thanks to Gabriella Oldham, super scholar and wonderful friend; Lou Forsdale, great teacher, friend, and wise counselor; Richard Admiral, master artist and superb storyteller; Lee Quinones, the king of the city; Nathan Glazer, expert and enthusiastic guide; Larry Greenstein, my best friend; and Mickey, Mia, and Ted Pearlman, to whom I pledge outstanding zeep.

To Henry Chalfant, Martha Cooper, Lynn Forsdale, Gabriella Oldham, Ted Pearlman, and Yolanda Rodriguez, the wonderful photographers who contributed their work for this book, my enduring gratitude.

At the MTA, thanks to Trudy Mason, Richard Ravitch, Reggie Lewis, Lou Collins, Gene Eisenhamer, Tom Pope, Art Harrington, Steve Polan, Jimmy Peters, and everybody else.

At the Transit Police Department, thanks to Morris Bitchachi, Theodore Rotun, Michael Bianco, Edward Silverfarb, and, especially, to Kevin Hickey and Conrad Lesnewski who are truly great cops (and ought to have gold shields).

At Columbia University, thanks to Jon Kowallis, John Payne, Penny Thrasher, Tim Vaca, Tony and Valerie Mauriello, Justin Schorr, William Mahoney, Robert Holloway, Louis Starr, Alan Walker Read, Alexander Alland, and Butler Library.

In Boston, thanks to my wonderful friends Neil Devins, Jan Ellis, and Gary Heiman.

At The MIT Press, my heartfelt thanks to everyone.

And, of course, special thanks and regards to Stan 153, Wicked Gary, Noga Jack, Fred, Tracy 168, Mitch, P-Body, Mad, Part, Rat, Candy, Daze, Jae 5, Slick, Adom 2, Chino Malo, Son I, Lee 163, Apollo, Carmen, Luz, Bloodtea, Scorpio, Duro, Seen, Dust, Ali, Zephyr, Caine, Rib, Revolt, Crash, Rasta,

Chad, Deal, Rammelzee, Kase, Wasp, Jester, KC-3, Teen, Slave, Slug, Mono, Doc, Cliff 179, Blade, Passion, P-Nut, Phase II, Stay High 149, T-Rex, Caz, Luce, IN, Sin, IOU One, PJay, Kathy 97, Mark, Cuda, PB 5, DEA 2, Barbara and Eva 62, Keno, Topcat 007, Taki 183 . . . AND ALL THE WRITERS.

*Whole car by Paze and Fome
dedicated to Pancho and Anita.*
Martha Cooper

*A typical writer's self-portrait with
shades and marijuana-leaf shirt.*
Martha Cooper

Lee's "Stop the Bomb" whole car.
Henry Chalfant

A typical holiday celebration whole car. "Merry Christmas" by PJay and Lyndah. Martha Cooper

Detail from Fred's "Cambell's Soup Pop Art" whole car. *Martha Cooper*

A Vaughan Bodé cartoon character reproduced on an IRT train. Unsigned. *Martha Cooper*

Getting Up

1

Interview with Lee of the Fabulous Five

Lee:

Here's how the whole train came into the picture. I told Slug that I had this idea about doing ten whole cars and Slug said, "Yeah, that's funny, I had that same idea." So I said, "Yeah, one night we gotta get together and do it." We got together a couple of nights, but we didn't get to do it. He got sick or he didn't want to go. It wasn't really fully down. So one night me and Mono talked about it.

Craig:

Tell that story.

Lee:

Yeah, that story. That's the greatest part of the whole Fab Five thing. One night I was in my house; I always had my drawer packed with paint. Mono came in and Mono said, "I'm gonna start racking up real strong this week. We're gonna do a whole train." I said, "What?" "We're gonna do a whole train! Ten cars. Me and you. Because these suckers are full of shit even though they're part of the Fabulous Five." So I said, "Yeah, man? Bet, man. I'm down. All right." Slave was there and Slave said, "You guys gonna do a whole train?" We said, "Yeah, we're gonna do it." So he said, "Yo, let me get down, let me do one. I'll do a car, and you two do the rest." So we said, "All right, bet." So we had three guys. Doc and them, they could've done it because they had paint themselves. They had closets full of paint. But at the time, Doc didn't wanna get down 'cause he thought we weren't really gonna do it. He thought it was impossible. But me and Mono had a feeling it could be done if you'd just stay in the lay-up and keep on nonstop. So we kept on every day, me and Mono, racking up, picking out the colors we need for outlines and fill ins. We planned out all the cars, one by one on paper, planning the amount of paint for each car, and it's funny, it was such a perfect job, a Dillinger job. It was so beautiful.

Going down to the details, we had to get at least 110 cans for this whole train. We got it in less than a week and a half. We just kept on racking it up. Slave already had his paint so he didn't have to rack up much. Me and Mono were the ones who had to do the hard work.

So finally we got together the night before we were gonna do it. And we said, "O.K. Let's pack up the paint and go ahead and do it." So we got the food ready, we racked up the fat caps, and we got the bags packed. We had a suitcase full of paint and so many shopping bags. Then the night came. We were at Doc's house on Staten Island and everybody was getting drunk except Mono and me. We couldn't get drunk 'cause that was the night we were going to do it. Doc and all of them were drunk and they were with their girls and they were making a lot of noise. So we said, "See you people." And Doc said, "Where you going?" And we said, "We're doing the whole train." Doc said, "Raahfuckyoubullshit!" And the girls were laughing and they were all buggin' out. So me and Mono looked at each other and we said, "Let's go." We had to run to get the ferry because it only runs once an hour. We were timing this. We had to be in the lay-up at around 9 o'clock at night, perfect. We got to my house and Slave came over. I kissed my mom goodbye. My mother already knew what we were going to do. And I said, "Mom, if we come back, you'll know what we did." So we got the paint ready, we went and paid our fares and took the train. We sat in separate cars. We each sat with our own stack of paint, and we were all praying that Hickey and Ski wouldn't walk in through those doors and say, "Aaahh! How you doin'?" You know, the cops. So we got to the lay-up, perfect. We were gonna do it in a lay-up that was far apart from everything but it wasn't there. So we did it in another lay-up that I didn't like. So we went there and the lights were on. Wow! The lights were on! I didn't like being there. Mono said, "Don't worry about it," but I was worried about it and I didn't want to do it so I said, "Let's go home." But Mono said, "You crazy? We got all this paint here and you wanna go home? You crazy after we did all this work?" So I said, "Ah fuck it man, we're gonna do it."

I had studied for this whole train for a few nights and I knew how it was gonna be lined up. I was gonna have a car, Mono was gonna have a car, Slave was gonna have a car, then another Mono, then a car that said the Fabulous Five with a Mickey Mouse, then a Lee whole car, but we gave that car to Slave. We said, "You do another car," and we gave him the paint for it. And then I was gonna do another whole car, and then we were gonna do the Christmas cars, two whole cars. I think that adds up to ten cars. I ended up doing six myself. So when we got to the lay-up, I already knew which colors would go with each car all the way from the first to the tenth. So we took all the paint, and we went inside the first car with the lights on and threw the paint all over the floor. 110 cars all over the place. The first car was mine so I picked out cascade green, faded with blues. So I took the colors, and put them on top of the seat, and we took the rest of the cans and went into the next car. We put the colors for that car on top of the seat and went into the next car. We did that all the way to the last car, with a certain amount of paint for each car stacked on the seats. Then we got the caps ready, put on gloves, and we said, "O.K. Let's start."

Everybody took their cans and we went outside and we started piecing. I did my first car in less than an hour. I was bombing. The colors were coming out and it burned. Mono and Slave were still on theirs. So I went down to start on my red piece and then after that to work on the Mickey Mouse. I finished my red piece. By then it was late at night, but we had plenty of time left and I started doing Mickey Mouse. So I was working on the Mickey Mouse, Slave had just finished his piece, and Mono was just starting a new one. Then all of a sudden Mono was next to me and he had his hands in my face and he was shouting, "Move, move!" And I said, "What's the matter?" but I answered my own question when I looked behind him, and I seen big flashlights. So I turned and I shouted, "Slave, Slave," and he was gone in a cloud of dust. He was gone. Mono tripped and fell on the floor; then he got up and started running toward the end of the train. I got under the train and there was another train pulling in next to it that almost hit me. I rolled as far from the moving train as I could, and I had a can of Ferro-Safety Purple in my hand and I threw that under the other train. So under the train I saw these big feet moving, shoes, and I said, "Oh no, cops, I knew it, I knew it." So I ran back to the other end of the train and Mono came out from where he was hiding and waved to me. At first, I didn't know who he was 'cause it was so dark, but then he came over and we were saying, "Cops, cops." So we watched and they climbed into the trains.

Now what we didn't know at this time was that they weren't cops; it was Doc, Slug, and Blood. They were fooling around. Doc was white, so he looked like a cop, a cop I knew named O'Leary with blond hair and a mustache. So Doc leaned out the window and shouted, "There they go." There was this black cop who'd been after us, Bubble-Lip, a husky guy . . . Grant, that's it, that's his name and Slug looked a little like him. Slug was big and husky, and he was far away and I looked and what I saw was Grant and O'Leary. So I shouted, "Mono, the cops!" So they started running toward us shouting "Freeze, you mother-fuckers!" But it was from a real distance, far away and all you could hear was them screaming, coming toward us. So I said, "Mono, the cops, the cops!" So Mono came out from inside the train and he came running toward me saying, "Let's get the way out of here." I left him in the dust. I ran up a staircase and when I got to the upper level, I tripped and fell on the third rail and I could hear the cops behind me and then Mono jumped over me, but he stopped and helped me up and we ran down the track to a place where you could get out through the fence. But it was dark there, and I was trying to find the hole, the little part that you open up. And I'm saying, "Damn. Where is it? Where is it?" and all the time these flashlights are getting closer and closer and I'm yelling, "Mono, find it, find it." Mono's going, "Shit, I can't find it," and we're getting all dirty, and dust is falling from the fence and we couldn't find it, but then suddenly I found it, the hole. And I pushed myself up and said, "Mono, jump," but he was saying, "Where are you? Help me! Help me!" And the lights all this time are getting closer like a suspense movie, and we could hear these voices saying, "You motherfuckers, we've got you now." And we didn't know that was Slug. "Yo, Mono, reach out, reach out." He couldn't see me. I could see him through a dim light, but he couldn't see me

Lee posing in front of his "Graffiti 1979" mural on a handball court on the Lower East Side.

'cause I was in the dark, but I said, "Mono, just reach out straight," and he caught my hand and I pulled him up and he said, "Let's get out of here." And we reached up to go out the grate but the grate was closed. So I said, "Oh, shit, it's jammed. Mono, we gotta get out of here, let's break out." So both of us jumped up—it was kind of high above us—at the same time and with our fists. We hit the grate and knocked it open, and we came out and there were some people standing there waiting for a bus and they looked at us coming out from the sidewalk all dirty and with our hands bleeding from the cuts across our knuckles from hitting the grates. And then these voices came up from the tunnel, and we ran. Bang, we were gone!

We ran through the streets all through Brooklyn. We ran all the way to the Williamsburgh Bank and that's a long way from Coney Island. Then we said, "Oh, man, this is fucked up; we only got half a train. We can't finish it. What are we gonna do?" We were walking through Tomahawk turf and all these guys looking at us real bad and we're the only Puerto Ricans around and I was scared but Mono said, "Don't worry about it; if they come for us, we'll run." We were talking so much we didn't notice how far we were walking. All the way down to the tip of Brooklyn. Mono said, "We're coming back man, cops or no, "You're crazy, Mono, I never return to lay-ups where I get raided." But he said, "Yo, we're coming back. We planned this shit out, we're gonna finish it. No matter what. Tomorrow night I'm bringing a knife. And if a cop comes up to me, I'll stab the nigger." And I said, "No, Mono, I'm not coming back." He said, "You're coming back." And I said, "Fuck it; I am."

So we went back to Staten Island, and Doc and them wasn't there. So we asked the girls, "Where's Doc?" And they said, "Aw, they went out somewhere." They'd gotten drunk; that's why they were fooling around with us. There was a big empty bottle of Night Train. Early in the morning, they came in and woke us up and I said, "Doc, we got raided last night." And he said, "Yeah?" And I said, "Yeah, it was fucked-up. The cops chased us." And he was smiling. And I said, "Yo man, what's the matter with you? I planned this shit out for months and you're laughing at me like you're crazy." And he said, "You know what? I liked your first piece. It was Cascade Green with blues." And I said, "How do you know that? That train didn't pull out yet." And he said, "I know it didn't pull out yet. I was there last night. How'd you like the raid?" And I said, "What?" And I grabbed him around the throat and I said, "I'll kill you!" We're crashing around the house and then he ran out the door and I chased him shouting, "I'll kill you!" Then Mono grabbed me and threw me on the floor. And he said, "What are you doing?" And I said, "These are the jerk-offs that raided us." And he said, "I know, I know. I wanna kick his ass too." And Slug is out in front of the house, laughing and shouting, "I liked your Mickey Mouse, ha, ha!" And I ran after him but I couldn't catch him. And I was mad.

That same night we went back and I was still a little afraid, but it was funny. We found the lay-up exactly as it was; paint cans were still there. My camera and everything was still there. The suitcase, my mother's suitcase, was still there. And that was good, I didn't want to lose that. The train was all dirty on the inside, sand and all, so this time we brought a broom with us to clean it up. Slave didn't come with us that night 'cause we couldn't find him. So we brought Doc and we said, "Doc, you finish up Slave's car." So Doc went right over the Slave piece. Slave had just started the piece so Doc said, "I've got no choice, I've just got to go over it." So he went over it, but it was an ugly Doc—it messed up the whole train.

So I finished the Mickey Mouse and it came out beautiful, just the way I planned. Then I started work on another car with a desert scene. And Mono finished his piece and then we all came together to start doing the rest. I was so tired. The first night, when we started doing it, I was energy packed. I was only drinking soda; Mono and Slave were drinking beer and stuff. But I was only drinking soda and eating crackers, and it was giving me energy and I could have painted all night. Since I got chased that night, a lot of that energy went into my feet. And with all that worry I lost a lot of energy, and I could piece but I couldn't piece as fast and as nice. So it was late when we got to the last two cars. And we said, "Let's leave them." But Mono said, "We're doing ten cars. We came here for ten cars and we're doing them. Fabulous Five!" So we did the Christmas cars. They were coming out nice but I was getting tired. And the thing is, they went inside and slept and left me out there by myself, piecing. Lazy bums, they were all high and I finished the two cars. But I finally finished and then I knocked on the window and I said, "Yo, Mono, it's finished." So we started packing up. Before that, Mono and I had been fighting over a can, I don't know what color it was, but we were fighting out between the cars. And we looked down at the same time and there was a work bum looking right at us. But this trackman, he just looked at us, and kept on walking. And we said, "Oh, shit, we're gonna get raided." But he just kept on walking and never came back. He never bothered us. He knew what we were doing because he must have smelled the paint and all. But that was one cool dude because he didn't tell nobody. He didn't tell no cops and no other workers because we stayed there for another three hours and nobody ever came. I guess he didn't give a hell what we were doing; he was an old guy.

Anyway we got out of the lay-up at six o'clock in the morning. At seven o'clock the lay-up was gonna pull out. So I went home, didn't sleep. Cleaned up just a little bit. Got my camera and went back to the station. At about seven o'clock I got there to Brooklyn Bridge and guys are coming up to me and they're shouting, "Oh man! Oh man!" And I said, "What's the matter with you?" And they said, "Oh man, I've seen it!" And I said, "What have you seen?" And they said, "A whole train!" All the writers were there for early morning rush. And they said, "It's bad style, Lee!" And I said, "Oh, shit, where is it?" And they said, "It went to the Bronx." So I got on the next train and I said, "I'm going after it. I don't want anybody with me." But I looked down at the next car and everybody got in. I said, "Oh no, they're following me."

So I got up to the Concourse, and the doors open and I got out the car and everybody said, "There goes Lee." And Butch, and one-armed Kase was there and they said, "Yo,

Lee, you're crazy, you're crazy!" And I sai
pened?" They said, "It's bad! It went upt
back on the train and they said, "We gotta u
bad." And I said, "Don't worry about it, we'll do one u
night," and the doors closed. And I went uptown.

It was a cold day. It was two weeks before Christmas. It was very cold that day. And we were at Intervale on the 5 and 2 waiting for that train. There were two fine girls waiting at the train station. And then the train was coming. And I said, "Look at that train." Like you could see barely on the side of it, all the colors flashing out toward the sun. The sun was right on them. And I said, "There it goes!" I got out my camera and it was coming closer and I said, "THERE IT GOES!" And it's coming closer with the cars swinging. And I said, "It's coming! It's coming!" And the girls are saying, "What's coming? What's coming?" And I said, "Look," and they said, "Oh my God!" And the first cars came in like a roaring horse and I said, "Look at it! Look at it!" And I was going so crazy I forgot to take pictures. And Devil who was with me said, "The pictures!" So I started taking pictures but I only grabbed like four cars. And then the train was pulling out so then I jumped on. And I looked back at the girls, and they were just standing there with their mouths open. And it was like crazy, like you could see the reflection in their eyes.

We decided to take the train to Baychester station and when the train stopped we'd pull the emergency cord to stop the train. That's our specialty. So when the train pulled in, BOOM, we pulled it and I took some photographs. Then we got between the cars. It was by coincidence that a train pulled in on the other side that was jam packed and it discharged all its passengers. They were taking it out of service. So that whole side of the station was packed and I know that it was a shock to all these Wall Street Journals with their classy suits and suitcases. And they saw the whole train and everybody's going like, "Oh, shit!" I'm looking out from between the cars and everybody's going, "Look at that," and I see all these hands pointing. Brooklyn Bridge is like lighted up for the first time. I was between the cars and people were looking at me but they didn't know who I was, but I said, "How do you like it, people?" And young students and people like us are saying, "Yeah, it's bad, all right!" It was beautiful, it was like a display and they were saying, "Oh, shit!" There was a whole bunch of people and there was a perfect crowd to see it and as the train was leaving, we stuck our heads out and we're shouting, "Yeah, Fabulous Five!" There were writers there and they said, "Look at them." We took it to 42d. On the way there we were really hauling ass and as we passed through the stations going fast the people were going, "Oh shit, Look at that" and pointing. At every station, it was a train stopper, a show stopper. At 14th Street, people were yelling and cheering, but 42d Street was the biggest. Everybody was going, "Wow, look at that, man!" It was slowing down so they saw it car by car. I know that Mickey Mouse must have blown everybody's mind. I started arguing with this black man. He didn't like it; it was surprising. He was prejudiced or something. I said, "How do you like it? It's a whole train." And he said, "Aah, it's disgusting." So I said, "Fuck you, you mother. If you don't like it it's too bad, because it's here right now." At 59th, the people saw it, at 86th there wasn't a big crowd, but at 125th, wow! It stopped right up to the platform so that you didn't get a long view, you had to walk in right through the pieces. The station was packed and people were walking into the pieces with their eyes open like wow, man. It was bad. It was nice to have it pull up right in front of you and then to get inside of it with the windows all painted. They probably didn't know it was graffiti; they probably thought the city was doing something good for a change. They probably thought they paid some muralist to do it.

When we went into the slums in the Bronx, the train was elevated so people could see the whole train. You could see people blocks away going, "Look at that!" I'm serious. I notice people, I watch people on the street. People only look up once in a while. They look down mostly. But this time, you'd see people looking up and they'd really look. Little kids were going, "Mickey Mouse. Look Mommy!" People were going crazy. There's a park at Simon Street where it makes a turn and there's a big avenue there, Westchester Avenue. People were all crowded up there in front of the stores, and they were looking up and going "Wow!" You could see the reflection in the windows of the slums of the cars all painted. Every car was like a TV, and you could see the colors reflected. And then we got to Baychester. The train was swinging from side to side. We were hanging out the sides and the windows going, "Yaah! Fabulous Five!" I was on the side of the train, I'd actually climbed out a little on the side and before the train stopped I jumped out onto the rocks and got to the other side, no matter what, cops or not, and took pictures. And then I heard the train go "whoosh" and it stopped and I knew they pulled the emergency. And then I heard the conductor going, "Who the hell pulled that?" Then I saw all the Fab Five jumping out of the train shouting, "Yaah, take pictures!" And everybody's there with their 35s, clicking. It was a nice sunny day. And when the train left, we said, "Yeah, all right. Job well done!" There was only one guy in that station, and he was looking at us. And I said, "How do you think about it?" And he said, "Incredible, man, incredible!" We didn't wait for it to come back. We decided to take the next train home.

It didn't run again. The next day I went to Brooklyn Bridge and I thought, "This thing has to be together. At least five cars." But they were all broken up. One train came in with Mickey Mouse, another came in with a Mono car, and I said, "Wow, split up already, oh my God!" Every piece was on different lines, different trains. It was crazy. But that had been the greatest moment of the Fab Five ever. And that I ever had.

Craig:

Would you describe each of the ten cars?

Lee:

Starting with number 1, a Lee top-to-bottom. It was Cascade Green. I used pound cans. That's hard to find, those cans with sixteen full ounces. A heavy-duty can. And a little bit of baby blue, and a Fed purple 3-D with red. And then an orange cloud with white shine. The second was a Mono blue top-to-bottom with National Blue 3-D and

*"Merry Christmas to New York," from
the Fabulous Five's Christmas Whole
Train.* Henry Chalfant

*"We have finally succeeded," from the
Christmas Whole Train.* Henry Chalfant

Spanish Brown clouds. The next car was a Slave, it was Hot Rod Gray and it had chains on it, little black chains, and it had a wizard on the other side with a green cap with stars and all and a yellow beard. That was bad. The next car was a Mono piece, a regular style top to bottom with a Schoolbus Yellow strip through it and Colonial Ivory on the other side. And then a nice red 3-D. And there was a city background with Marlin Blue sky with a guy trucking through it pointing down the train, and then one car away was my car with a guy pointing the other way toward him, with both of them pointing toward the main car, "The Fabulous Five" with Mickey Mouse right dead in the middle. And it said, "The Fabulous Five" in nice plain letters with colors like rainbows coming out. Like the whole car was full of colors. Then there was my Lee in red with a white 3-D with a man trucking and the city in the background. And then came a Doc, it was a weird Doc. It said "Doc, Fab Five" with Dune Tan and Delta Blue. I forget the 3-D color, I think it was black. The next car was one of my pieces with Ferro Safety Green with a dark green 3-D with black trim. It was a scene of a desert with a guy with a horse, no, a donkey. It was pulling a wagon, like an old Western cowboy scene. And he was looking at a piece on a billboard in the middle of the desert. Then the last two cars were me, Mono, and Doc together. Christmas cars with Santa Claus and reindeer and snow, the snow was falling. And there were Christmas trees in the background and a snowman. The pieces were nice and it was a great feeling to do those last cars.

That was the greatest thing we ever did and I think it was the greatest thing ever done on the IRT number 4 train. It was a big show stopper and I think those people who saw it went home that night and didn't watch TV. They talked about the train they saw.

We had so much fever we planned another one for the next week but we didn't get to do it. This one was going to be an animated train with all the famous cartoons—Dick Tracy, Popeye, a lot of cartoons that are real famous. We were going to do a face on the front of the train, except for the conductor's window and the front window, we were going to do a face, smiling. And Slug said, "Let's do both sides. Both sides, and the top." I said, "Wow!" To do that, you'd need a good lay-up and a lot of time. Be nice if we could get permission to paint one train on a famous line with a lot of people, like the A train or D train. Even if we could get a work train or a money train, they're about ten cars, we could draw cops and robbers on the money train. It might happen but by the time the MTA knows what graffiti is, it might be too late.

Craig:

Would you describe each member of the Fabulous Five?

Lee:

Mono is basically Puerto Rican. He's Puerto Rican; he's got a mustache, a beard, a DA, blue eyes; he's big—a little fat now from drinking too much beer. That's basically Mono. He's got a temper, a very hard temper. But he's cool. He's always cool in the trains. He's the quietest guy out of the whole Fabulous Five. When me and him used to go by ourselves it would be quiet. We'd do our pieces and then walk out.

Doc. He's a very tall guy, almost seven feet, real tall. He has to bend down to get through the doors, and he always wears a big green army jacket and he's got a mustache and a blond DA and he's tall. He can run like there's no tomorrow.

Slug is a black guy. He's husky, walks bowlegged and he's philosophical, he's smart. He's weird. When he talks he goes down to details. Everything. He's been to college and all that. He sued the city in '60-something. He got hit by a train on the head. You know Bowling Green station? Near South Ferry? The train comes around a sharp turn and one day there was a thing, a sharp object, sticking out of the train, a big metal thing, a window wiper or something. It hit him right in the head, and it mixed him up a little. He's kind of absent-minded but you can't blame him. One minute he's just talking and the next minute he wants to fight with you. He thinks the same way graffiti-wise. He's very smart in the lay-ups, he knows everything. He's calm when raids come, planning which way to go.

Slave, the tall guy, cool and quiet, very quiet. Quiet everywhere he goes. Brooklyn writer. He's skinny, has a big head. Slave is all right. He's cool.

I stayed on top, still doing trains. But they were going down too fast. They dropped. And I stayed floating. I'm still floating.

2

Writing

Ted Pearlman

Getting Up

Style, form, and methodology, major concerns of most writers, are secondary in significance to the prime directive in graffiti: "getting up." The term has been used by writers since the mid-1970s. Before that time other terms, including *getting around*, *getting over*, and *getting the name out*, were used to signify the same idea. Regardless of the term used, however, since the beginning writers have understood that recognition and acceptance of their work by other writers (and possibly the public in general) is dependent on their writing their names prolifically.

Hugo Martinez, director of the United Graffiti Artists organization, saw this emphasis on getting up as one of the more significant factors differentiating New York's subway writers from the creators of traditional forms of wall writings. Martinez has stated that "the significant feature of the new graffiti is its sense of purpose, the particular emphasis it places on 'getting around.' Only a youth with a sense of vocation can put in the necessary amount of work."[1]

The magnitude of this enterprise can come as a surprise to a new writer. Lee, a Manhattan writer, reacted with shock when he was first introduced to the concept of getting up. Flea I, Lee's graffiti teacher, took Lee into an underground train lay-up in the Bowery to show him how and where graffiti is written. Lee, fearing arrest, was reluctant to go in, but he steeled his nerves and went into the dark tunnel prepared to do a single black and gold "piece" that he was sure would bring him lasting fame. It was then that he learned the "awful truth." Lee recalled the incident in an interview:

> So he took me to this place and he said, "You know after you do this you have to keep doing it." I said, "What?" I said, "No, man!" I thought you just do it once and you're famous, you've got your name all over. How stupid could I be. One train! You'd only see it once in a lifetime, there's so many of them. I didn't realize then how many trains there was in this city. So he said, "You've got to keep doing it if you want to get up." And I said, "Wow, man." And I was worried like hell . . . but I did it . . . and I went back again . . . and I kept on and kept on.

Today Lee appears to be respected and admired by all of the writers in the city. P-Body calls Lee's style "the best in the city. And man, he gets up!"

Style is important to writers. By demonstrating a good sense of design and a facility with the use of spray paint, a writer can win the esteem of other writers and even that of some members of the public. However, as Tracy 168 has said, "Style don't mean nothing if you don't get up. If people don't see your pieces, how are they gonna know if you've got style?"

Writers are more than willing to overlook deficiencies in the style of a person who is known to be up a lot. The coveted title of king of the line goes to the writer who gets up the most on a particular subway route, regardless of style. Writers even manage to overlook the abysmal style of IN's "throw-ups" and acknowledged him as king of all the lines because, ugly as they were, thousands of them appeared on the trains.

Cliff 179 was painting high-status "whole cars" from his first days in graffiti, but his style was not "too swift," and he won little respect from his fellow writers until they noticed that he was getting up a lot. Today his style has improved greatly, but he won his fame from his high rate of productivity. Caz and Fred discussed this matter in an interview:

Fred:

Some of the early Cliff pieces, they were pretty sick. All of us writers in Brooklyn really hated his stuff. It was weird looking. His stuff always dripped.

Caz:

His stuff might have dripped but it was out there. That's what counts. No matter how sloppy it was, it was around.

Fred:

That's what used to amaze me about Cliff. The first time I saw it I said, "This guy is no good." But then you saw this same guy all over everywhere and you said, "He really gets around!" I thought his style was bad, but it got so drummed into my head that I just came to appreciate it for what he wanted to do and how he wanted to express himself.

Form is important to writers. As the forms of subway graffiti increase in size and complexity from simple marker "tags" to enormous, spray-painted whole cars, there is a corresponding rise in the status that accompanies them. Adopting a high-status form will not bring a writer fame, however, unless he manages to get up a lot with it. Whole-car painters are not expected to do as many works as those who adopt other forms, and they can win recognition with as few as twenty well-styled efforts. "Taggers" on the other hand, according to Keno, Son I, and other full-time devotees of the form, have to write their names at least a thousand times before they can expect to be noticed by the other writers.

With a few exceptions, writers are considered to have retired once they stop writing, and they are forgotten quickly by most of the writers who are still active. In order to maintain a reputation in the graffiti world, a writer must manage to get up continually. Blade, Jester, and Wasp have retired a number of times but stage frequent comebacks in order to keep their names alive.

Blade is now twenty-three years old and currently is engaged in his fourth comeback attempt. He has been getting up a lot recently with big, "end-to-end," "BLADE IS BACK!" pieces, painted in geometrical letters that he has dubbed "robot style." Blade is aware of the fact that as an adult, he is subject to a charge of malicious mischief and a possible year's term in jail if he is caught writing, but, as his friend Tracy 168 has said of him, "If he's gonna stay on top, he's got to keep getting up."

Style

Every writer would like to be known as having good style, and most writers devote long hours to practicing piece design in sketch pads and notebooks. Many writers also spend a great deal of time sitting in subway stations watching and criticizing the pieces that go by, passing around their sketches, and "autographing" each other's "black books" (hardbound sketch pads that almost all writers carry with them). Many writers put a great deal of care into these autographs, and a writer who does an exceptionally fine drawing in one of them is said to have "burned the book." A "burner" in an autograph book reflects well on both the artist and the owner of the book.

Impressive though it may be, however, style in the books does not count for much among the writers. The style that one displays on the trains means the most. Almost any experi-

Burner by Lace. Lynn Forsdale

Wild-style piece. Henry Chalfant

3-D piece by Mad and Seen.
Lynn Forsdale

enced writer can design a good piece, but translating that de-sign into a painting on the side of a train is far different.

In order to create a burner on a train, a writer must have a good sense of design, a masterful spray-painting technique, and the ability to work carefully and diligently in the difficult conditions of the train yards and under the constant threat of capture. Writers look upon the creation of burners on the trains as an example of true grace under pressure, and those who consistently get up with style are admired for both their skill and their bravery.

Long before they attempt to paint on trains, young writers will develop their style through practice in sketch pads and often on walls around their neighborhoods. They also will fre-quently seek out more experienced writers to teach them the ropes. Young writers who do not have the skill or talent neces-sary to create designs of their own will often ask more skillful friends to "give" them styles. "Master" writers will frequently have one (perhaps a younger brother) or even a large group of young protégés whom they will bring along. Writers seem to enjoy the role of teacher and take pride in the accomplish-ments of their students, as well as take pleasure in the admiration and respect they receive from them. Both Bama, a famous writer from the early 1970s, and Tracy 168, an equally famous writer of a later period, take pride in the success of their teacher-student relationship and remain close friends to this day.

Even some experienced writers have never mastered the creation of style. These writers will sometimes seek assistance from more skillful colleagues, but more often they will simply watch the trains and borrow, or "bite," other writers' styles. Biting is looked down upon by most writers, and those who are bit will often become angry and seek out the biter for a con-frontation or even a fight.

Bama, a writer whose unique styles were frequently bor-rowed by others, takes a philosophical attitude toward biting: "A lot of writers would get angry if their style was bitten. Get angry and go over there and yell, scream, punch. 'You took my style, man; what's wrong with you!' 'But I just saw you doing it.' 'I don't care what the fuck you saw, you don't ever steal my style!' But I don't want to hit anybody in the head. . . . I always took it as a compliment that other people liked my style that much." Tracy 168 takes a philosophical, if somewhat more practical, view of biting: "I don't care who uses my style. As long as they pay me for it."

Writers are keen critics of each other's styles. When they judge the merits of a piece, they generally look for originality of design, a smooth integration (called "flow") of letters, brightness of color, smoothness of paint application (black spots and, especially, drips are abhorred), sharpness and accuracy of outlines, and the effective use of details (decorations that are frequently worked into the letters of the name, ranging from simple lines, swirls, arrows, and stars to highly complex caricatures and other drawings). When writers spot a piece that exhibits poor design or technique, they will simply say "bad style," frequently backing up this contention with a detailed analysis of the piece's flaws. When a well-executed and finely styled piece is seen, writers employ any of a number of terms to show their approval. Since most writers see themselves as "outlaw" artists, many of the terms of approval have a seemingly negative ring. Among the strongest of these terms are "nasty," "the death," "vicious," "bad," and "dirty." Other terms of approval include "the joint," "juicy," "down," "down with the crew," "burner," "on," and "snap."

Since most writers like to think of their styles as being original and unique, they also like to invent names for them. When Mitch painted his name in old-fashioned Western-style letters, he called it his "Saloon Letter Piece." He has also done "Hot Dog Letter," "Earthquake Letter," and numerous other-lettered pieces. There are literally hundreds of style names in use by writers around the city, but they are rarely remembered by anyone but the artists who create them. The only style names that are in general use are "bubble letter," fat, rounded letters that were designed and named by Phase II; "3-D letter," block letters with a three-dimensional appearance, first used by Pistol I; and "wild style," a name used to describe almost any "unreadable" style. There is substantial disagreement among writers as to who first coined the term *wild style*. One writer stated that "it was some guy who lived 'way up in the Bronx who thought it up first. He went crazy later on. I think he's dead now." Tracy 168, though he does not completely match this description, has stated that he first used the term and now heads a group called the Wild Styles.

Writers who do not possess a gift for the creation of style names simply name their designs after themselves. Such names as "Chino Malo style" or "the style of Tean" help to point out their creators' views of their styles as being wholly personal and are also easy for others to remember.

Fred feels that the wide concern with style names is not entirely appropriate or correct: "There is one main style and that is graffiti itself. When you see it, you know for certain reasons that it is graffiti and that makes all graffiti part of a single style: Subway Style. Graffiti Style."

Form

Although there are hundreds of individual styles of graffiti, there are only seven basic forms in which it appears. These forms, the names of which are known to all graffiti writers, can be distinguished generally by their size, location, complexity of design, or the materials used to create them. They are discussed here in ascending order of complexity.

Tags

Tags are the names written all over the insides of most New York subway cars. Most writers consider them to be the most basic and simplest form of graffiti. A tag generally consists of the writer's name in stylized letters that are gathered together somewhat in the style of a logo or monogram. Tags are written very quickly, often in a single, practiced movement, in a single color of ink or paint. In style, tags are about as individual as the writer's handwriting. Similarities among tags are basically a function of the tools used to create them.

Spray paint was the first tool employed for tagging, in the late 1960s, but it is rarely used today. Spray paint enables a writer to make a very large mark, but it is inconvenient for use inside the trains. It takes longer to apply and to dry than marker ink and also has a tendency to run and drip when used in close quarters, spoiling the writer's efforts to demonstrate a clean and controlled technique. The paint cans also give off powerful fumes that can attract the unwanted attention of passengers and conductors.

Niji and Dri-Mark pens were the first markers to come into general use in tagging. They had quarter-inch chisel tips and

Spray-paint tags inside an IRT car.
Lynn Forsdale

Marker and spray-paint tags.
Lynn Forsdale

were available in a wide variety of colors. They enabled writers to tag their names more quickly than had been possible with spray paint and were easily concealed when not in use. Their mark was disappointingly small, however, and when larger markers became available, the quarter-inchers were abandoned and dismissed as unacceptable "toy markers."

The most preferred tagging tool is the Uni (Uni-wide 200 is the brand name), a flat, refillable marker with a two-inch-wide tip. In tagging, a Uni is generally held with three fingers on top and the thumb below for maximum speed and ease of movement. A writer will sometimes split the tip of a Uni into a number of sections, inking each with a different color, and thereby enhancing the already wide and impressive mark of the pen by lending it a rainbow effect.

Because so many of these markers were stolen by writers in the past, stores in New York stopped carrying Unis years ago. Those still being used are either in the possession of "old writers" or are being used by younger writers who have inherited them from older brothers or friends who have retired from writing. Writers also pride themselves on their ability to make homemade markers out of schoolboard-eraser wicks and bodies made of soup cans, tobacco tins, lighter bodies, Absorbine Junior bottles, baby food jars, and other containers. For both actual Unis and homemade imitations, as well as for other refillable markers, writers use either Flowmaster ink or concoct their own from a variety of substances. In making ink, emphasis is placed on ineradicability.

After the Uni market dried up, a smaller, cheaper version of the pen was brought out by another manufacturer under the name Mini-Wide. Minis have a one-inch tip, are refillable, and are still available at certain disreputable candy stores around the city for about a dollar.

The most common marker used for tagging today is the Pilot, a long, cylindrical marker with a half-inch chisel tip. Pilots are refillable and practically indestructible and can be bought in almost any stationery or art-supply store. Their mark is not as impressive as that of a Uni or Mini, but they are easily available, simple to conceal, and, when the tip is softened with a pin and flooded with ink, it is capable of making a "juicy" mark. Any pen smaller than a Pilot is looked upon with contempt as a toy marker. Only when there are no ready alternatives will a graffiti writer resort to the use of a Flair or an El Marko.

Some tagging is done on moving trains. Writers will walk through a train until they find an empty car or one with only a few disinterested passengers. If no police officers or conductors are about, the writers will then tag their names quickly and move on to another car. Cool Herc was one of the few writers who was willing to write in crowded cars. Supposedly he politely asked passengers to lean forward for a moment, tagged on the walls behind them, reminded them not to lean back until the ink had a moment to dry, and them moved on to the next car. Most writers, though, prefer to do their tagging unobserved and usually do it at night, in train yards and lay-ups (places where trains are stored on unused tracks), moving swiftly through the empty, darkened trains.

Some writers have favorite spots in the cars where they prefer to write their tags. Wasp likes to write his name on the tips of the blades of overhead fans, Maze prefers writing on the motorman's doors, and Sin I and Sage usually write on the windows. The most popular areas in the cars on which to tag, however, are the large corner panels and the wide panels under the advertisements. In a pinch the maps will also do.

Perhaps because it is the most common and least challenging form of graffiti writing, tagging carries the least status of any of the forms. Many of the writers who specialize in painting larger works on the outsides of the trains look upon tags as ugly, worthless "scribble-scrabble" and think very little of the writers who create them. There is, however, a widely recognized and honored title, "king of the insides," which is granted to the person who does the most tagging on a particular line.

Throw-Ups

Throw-ups are the fastest and easiest way to get up on the outsides. A throw-up usually consists of a two- or three-letter name that is formed, usually rounded, into a single unit that can be sprayed quickly and with a minimum of paint on the sides of a train. Throw-ups are usually done in a modified bubble letter style consisting of thick, simplified letters, incom-

Throw-up by IOU One. *Ted Pearlman*

*SIN paints his throw-up on a junked
train in the Pelham train yard because,
as he explains in the box at the right,
there was "Not one [in-service] train in
site!" Ted Pearlman*

pletely painted in one color, and outlined inexactly with a second, darker color. The question of style is never raised with throw-ups, and the writers who paint them are judged not by their command of style but by the number of throw-ups they manage to get up on the trains.

Many writers who usually do their writing in one of the larger, more complex forms will also do an occasional throw-up just to keep their names visible between more impressive efforts. Dean, for example, will do a throw-up, using the name KO, whenever he finds that he lacks the time or sufficient paint to do a full piece.

True throw-up specialists like IN, TI, W-5, and Tee will often fill entire sides of cars with their throw-ups in their efforts to become well known. Usually a throw-up artist wins the title "king of the line," which is granted to the writer who gets his name up the most on the outsides on a particular subway line. Writers who win this honored title are generally respected by their peers for the enormity of their efforts, but no one ever compliments them on their style.

The term *throw-up* is also used to refer to writing done in other forms that is lacking in style. When used to describe anything but an intentional throw-up, the term has the same meaning as *bad style*.

Pieces

Pieces, short for "masterpieces," are the names, usually consisting of four or more letters, that are painted on the outsides of subway trains. Pieces are usually painted beneath the windows over a span of less than the total length of the car. Any piece that extends above the windows to the top of the car or is extended over its entire length enters a new category.

Top-To-Bottoms

Generally referred to as *T-to-Bs*, these are names, often accompanied by drawings and other backgrounds and decorations, that extend from the bottom of a subway car to its top but not the full length of the car. T-to-Bs are usually done by writers who do not have the time, the paint, or the energy to paint a whole car.

Two-tone "quick piece" by Zephyr.
Lynn Forsdale

Style of Crash piece by Crash.
Henry Chalfant

A color-blended burner dedicated, for her birthday, "Too Mom!" by Lee.
Henry Chalfant

"Henry" piece (dedicated to
photographer Henry Chalfant) and a
top-to-bottom drawing by Passion.
Henry Chalfant

End-to-Ends

End-to-ends are names and accompanying decorations that extend from one end of a subway car to the other. An E-to-E rarely consists of a single name and is generally used by those who wish to write their own names and those of friends. Often two writers share in the creation of an E-to-E, painting together and sharing materials in order that their names will appear as a single unified work.

Whole Cars

A whole car is an entire subway car painted from top to bottom and end to end, including the windows. On the average IRT car this is an expanse approximately twelve feet high and fifty feet long.

Whole cars are frequently painted by groups who share paint and skills and generally work from a plan drawn in advance that outlines the design and colors to be used. A great many cans of spray paint are used in the creation of a whole car—twenty is said to be the average—and writers often selectively "rack up" (steal) paint for weeks in preparation for a whole-car effort. When a whole car is done by a group, the most experienced writers will take on the task of preparing the preliminary drawings and painting the decorations and the outlines of the names. Less-skilled writers in the group paint backgrounds and fill in large areas. A group-painted whole car usually includes the names of individual group members, in the form of tags, at the bottom or the ends of the car. Any large, painted words are usually in the form of a title, a message, or the name of the writers' group.

A number of writers are capable of painting whole cars single-handedly. Lee, Mono, Doc, Slave, and Slug, members of the Fabulous Five group, all painted numerous individual whole cars during their writing careers. Almost all serious outside writers attempt at least one whole car, and a large number do them frequently.

In order to paint the upper areas of the car, writers attempt to find boxes or ladders to climb on. If none are available or if the writers are in a hurry to complete their work, they will jump up and grasp the rain gutter that runs over the doors, hanging onto it with one hand while painting with the other. To reach areas that lie well past the doors, the writers have to hang from a slight ridge that runs along the top of the car, bracing their feet on the small bolts that protrude from the car farther below.

To be able to create a whole-car burner is considered by most writers to be the epitome of style and skill, and those writers who achieve them are much admired.

Whole Trains

For a long time whole cars were considered by writers to be the highest possible form of subway graffiti. Over the last few years, however, a number of writers have painted even larger works. Slug, for example, once painted his name in such a way that it covered two entire adjoining cars. Lee has a number of two-car works to his credit, and Caine is known to have painted one of them as well. Such two-car murals are the largest works done thus far by individual writers. On two occasions, however, groups of writers have managed to paint entire trains from top to bottom and end to end. These gigantic works are known as whole trains or "worms."

Most writers agree that the first whole train was painted in the number 7 yard by Caine, Mad 103, and Flame One on the night of July 4, 1976. Titled "The Freedom Train," it consisted of eleven whole cars painted on bicentennial themes. A number of early versions of the American flag were depicted ("Don't Tread on Me," for example), and there was also a Puerto Rican flag, the current fifty-star flag, and a free-form stars-and-stripes car.

The day after the Freedom Train was completed, it was taken out of service, photographed by the Transit Police, and was not returned to the line until it was repainted. According to Lee, the writers who painted the train were informed on by some other writer, and the police picked them up in their homes the following day. Lee believes that the arrests of the writers and, especially, the destruction of their whole train, was ". . . stupid. They did something for the United States and somebody dropped a dime [informed] on them and they busted them."

The second whole train to be created was painted on two December nights in 1977 in the Coney Island yard by Lee, Mono, Doc, and Slave of the Fabulous Five. The ten-car train was dubbed "The Christmas Train" and featured a two-

*End-to-end piece by Partners in Crime
(Mad and Seen).* Lynn Forsdale

Whole car by Dust. Lynn Forsdale

39

Detail from a whole car by Lee.
Henry Chalfant

"Welcome to Hell" whole car by Caine.

car holiday scene depicting reindeer, Santa Claus, a snow-man, falling snowflakes, and the words "Merry Christmas to New York."

There are plans for future whole trains. Fred is considering returning from retirement to paint a pop art whole train that would feature entire cars painted on both sides and their tops to resemble loaves of Wonder Bread and other familiar commercial products. Cliff would like to paint a whole train that is one continuous cartoon strip. As for Lee, he considers the painting of the Christmas Train the greatest achievement of his long writing career and has said, "I told Mono and Doc, 'I'm always down [ready]. I'm down anytime to do it again.' I don't care how aged I am, how old, I'm down to do it again. And the next time, even better."

Messages

Not all graffiti writers are content simply to write their names. Many of them accompany their works with messages. Lee 163, one of the earliest graffiti writers, used to accompany his tags with rhymes—"I'm Lover Lee/Can't You See" was one—and lines drawn from "funkadelic" music like, "Free Your Mind and Your Ass Will Follow." Members of the Ex-Vandals group in Brooklyn used to accompany their tags with coded messages like "W.B.Y.A." ("We Bust Your Ass") and "W.N.O." ("We're Number One").

Today the most common messages that appear on the out-sides of the trains are writers' comments on their own pieces. If the painting has gone well, the writers may append messages to their pieces reading, "Freak Y'all!" "I Burned!" "I Always Get Up Good!" or "Graffiti Lives!" If pieces do not come out well, the writers may explain their realization of that fact by writing "Fucked Up" or "Bad Piece" on them, sometimes accompanying that comment with an explanation of the problem like, "It Rained," "Paint Fucked Up," "No Time to Burn," or "Got Chased."

Although writers tend to avoid writing on each other's pieces, a particularly good message may attract comments written by other writers. On a recent whole car depicting a policeman holding a club, the writer appended the message, "Pigs and Informers Can Go to Hell!" Beneath that someone else had written the words "Right On!" And below that the

Message on an end-to-end by Passion.
Henry Chalfant

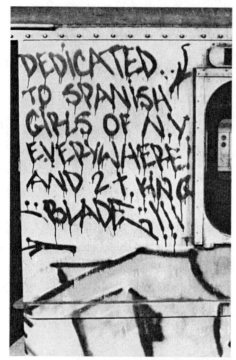

Teen dedicates a piece to "Spanish girls of N.Y. and 2 t. [to the] king . . . Blade!!!" Lynn Forsdale

Unsigned message. Henry Chalfant

tags of more than twenty writers appeared, all of them signifying their agreement with the original writer's message and the second writer's comment.

Lee is known for writing rather elegant messages to accompany his whole cars. Besides the "Hi Mom!" that he writes in the corner of each of his works, he also has written: "Tho Running Through All This Grime and Crime There Is Still Beauty in These Trains" and "I'm the Love Sick Bomber [meaning master writer] Just Surviving In New York City."

Some messages comment on current political and social issues. Lately antinuclear statements have predominated. Crunch accompanied one of his tags with the line "Use Your Heads Now or Lose Your Tails Later—Stop the Nukes!" Revolt and Zephyr accompany all of their pieces and tags with the words "No Nukes!" often surrounded by a drawing of a mushroom cloud.

Writers frequently dedicate their pieces to fellow writers or other friends or relatives or to popular public figures. Mono once dedicated a whole car to two graffiti squad officers, writing "This Is for Hickey and Ski."

At holiday times such messages as "Merry Christmas to All the Writers," or "Happy New Years Bronx!" are appended to many pieces. Birthdays are often celebrated in the same manner.

There is only one recorded case of a nonwriter getting into the act by adding his comments to a piece. As Caz tells it, he began work on a large piece one night but left before completing it when he heard a noise. He returned the following evening to finish the painting and found, "Just Missed You—Wait Till Next Time—the Watchman," written on it in large letters, with a ballpoint pen.

Backgrounding

Since the early days of subway graffiti there has been a code among the writers banning them from "backgrounding" (also called "going over" or "crossing out") each other's pieces. This code also states that once a piece has been "gone over" it is considered destroyed and becomes fair game for all other writers. Thus even the smallest cross-out can result in the eventual total elimination of a piece.

Duster crossed out in two colors by PJay. Ted Pearlman

Blade warns other writers: "I see you people like crossing out my pieces. If I see any more of my pieces crossed out I will 'Destroy All Pieces!'"

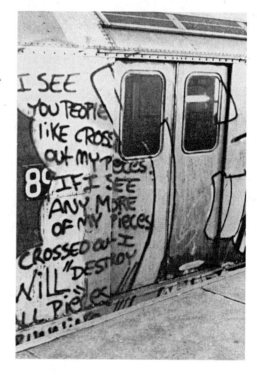

PJay whole car crossed out by the Outlaw Art group. Henry Chalfant

Backgrounding frequently takes the form of Xs or lines painted across the center of a piece. Sometimes a cross-out is accompanied by the name of the backgrounder or by an explanation of his motivation such as "Payback" (revenge for being crossed out himself) or "You Dropped a Dime [informed to the police] on Me."

Pieces by writers who are considered to be troublemakers, habitual backgrounders, or informers are sometimes backgrounded with the words "Hot 110." Although most writers are aware of the meaning of the term, its origins are unknown. Cross-outs can also take the form of art criticism, with writers painting "Toy Style," "No Style," or "Wacked Out" over works of which they do not approve.

Writers who are backgrounded usually will try to determine their offenders' identities and then will either confront them or retaliate by going over one of their pieces. This can escalate into a "cross-out war" with the antagonists, and sometimes their friends, crossing each other out for weeks or even, as was the case with Caz and Blade, for years until some sort of truce is called.

In 1978 the words "The Cross Outs" and the initials "TCO" began appearing over pieces painted on the IRT lines. TCO was rumored to be a group of "no-style writers" who took out their frustrations by backgrounding their more talented colleagues. Revenge was immediately sworn but no one could figure out who they were. Eventually TCO disappeared, but writers still occasionally speak of it. In retrospect many writers now believe that the police were behind TCO. Apollo 5 has explained this point of view. "It was the cops. They know the writers are like a family and they wanted to split us up." Tracy 168, who lost a whole car to TCO, has stated, "I don't know who did it but a lot of good pieces were lost. It was like someone going in the museum and ripping up all the art. A crime."

Racking Up

It is a tradition among most graffiti writers that all materials used in writing be stolen. The process of acquiring such materials is called "racking up." Racking up is like any other sort of shoplifting: the thief takes an object, hides it on his person, and gets out of the store as quickly and unobtrusively as possible. Writers often rack up as a team, with one person acting as a lookout or distracting the clerk while the other grabs the goods.

One of the most common methods of racking up paint is to hide it in the sleeves or down the front of a large ski parka or fatigue jacket. Such coats are baggy or puffy looking, and a number of cans can be hidden in them without causing any suspicious lumps that a clerk or store detective might notice. Because such clothing is winter wear, much of this sort of racking up is done during the colder months and extra paint is stockpiled for use during the summer. If more paint is needed during the summer, the most popular method of acquiring it is to "rack up in your socks," hiding the cans under a pair of baggy-legged trousers.

Some rackers are better than others, and those who are best at it will often take more paint than they can use, selling the excess to other writers who are less skilled at stealing or more timid about it. There is an active black market among the writers, and experienced rack-up artists like Keno and Chino Malo can turn a profit filling orders for other writers.

One of the most spectacular paint rack ups took place during the summer of 1972. Someone had knocked out part of a wall at an upper Manhattan high school in order to get into the storeroom. The thieves had taken whatever it was they wanted, not paint, and had gone away. Later that evening Jace 2 was passing by the school and saw the hole in the wall. Looking inside and seeing shelves full of paint, he hurried off and called his group, the Three Yard Boys, together. When they heard that there was paint to be had, they hurried to the school and carried out boxes and shopping bags full of paint. According to a former member of the group, Jace carried out 103 cans that night and the other members got even more.

Another spectacular rack-up, alleged to have taken place in the winter of 1977, was not the result of a chance discovery. According to police officer Kevin Hickey, three writers carefully planned and executed a late-night robbery at a warehouse in the Bronx, getting away with more than 2,000 cans of spray paint. Only Rustoleum and Red Devil paint, the brands most preferred by writers, were taken.

There have also been a few cases of "mass racking," in which a large group of writers have entered a store, grabbed paint, and then run out. Stan 153 has described one such incident: "Thirty-two of us get together and go to a Martin Paint store. We all walk in the door and the clerks are saying, 'Where are you guys going, what do you want?' 'Don't worry about it.' Everybody's looking around and somebody yells, 'There goes the paint! Run!' So we all run back and grab an armful of paint and then somebody shouts, 'Run! Run! He's gonna lock the door!' We got away with it, we got out O.K. Who's gonna try to stop thirty-two guys?"

Small markers, used in the black books, are easy to rack up. Wasp, an acknowledged rack-up artist, has developed a technique whereby he has only to take a marker from a display, hold it in his hand, and snap his fingers in order to have it disappear up his sleeve. Large markers used for tagging, however, are usually kept under the counter in stores, and the only possible way to steal them is "Bogarting." This method requires the rackers to convince a clerk to let them see a desired pen. When they have their hands on it, the writers look it over, usually say "thank you," and then run from the store as fast as they can. Because Bogarting yields only a pen or two at a time, requires a great deal of nerve, and exposes the thief to a greater risk of capture than more subtle methods, writers usually Bogart only enough large markers for themselves, and the pens rarely appear on the black market. Writers who are unwilling to hazard a Bogart attempt either to steal markers from each other or, though they would be loath to admit it, buy them.

In the Yards

Most graffiti writing is done at night at the numerous yards and lay-ups around the city where subway trains are stored. Writers climb over walls, go through holes in fences, and vault high gates in order to get into the yards. To reach lay-ups, they climb down from station platforms and "run the boards" (walk on the running board over the third rail) or move along narrow catwalks to get to the parked trains.

As an aid to the successful scheduling of a "yard trip," many writers memorize the locations and train-storage schedules of various yards and lay-ups. Transit police officer Conrad Lesnewski has stated:

> They know what time the trains pull in. They'll tell you, "The last train pulls in at 8:32 [at a lay-up], the first one pulls out on Monday morning at 6:43. At Utica Avenue on the lower level, the train pulls in at 9:17, but they don't lay up a train on that track on Thursday." They know all that from watching and watching and watching, time in and time out. . . . They'll see a new train leave from the yard on the lines, brand new just from the paint shop. They'll follow that train all day long and all night to see where it lays up and when that train lays up at a certain yard, they'll hit it before the night's over.

In the early days when writers traveled to the yards, they carried only a few cans of paint and some markers. Today they often bring food, drink, "smoke," radios, gloves, a change of clothes, and, if a particularly large piece is planned, suitcases or shopping bags full of paint.

Yards and lay-ups are dimly lit, and writers cannot risk attracting attention by using flashlights, so much of their work is done by "feel." Writers will frequently "break night" or even sleep in the yards in order to be able to take a good look at or photograph their pieces in daylight before the cars are moved or scrubbed.

Since there are hundreds of yards and lay-up points throughout the city, writers have a wide choice of places to do their work. They generally prefer to paint in the larger yards or in underground lay-ups where their chances of being detected are slightest. Most also prefer to work in yards where older trains, like those that run on the IRT lines, are stored. The older cars (writers call them "coalminers") have a surface that is much harder to clean than that of the newer stainless-steel cars (called "ding dongs" or "rocket trains") that are used on the IND and BMT lines. Pieces painted on the older cars tend to last longer, and as a result the largest and most spectacular pieces are painted on the IRTs, known to most writers as the "burning lines." Writers tend to avoid any yard or lay-up that is rumored to be "hot," meaning that the police have arrested or chased writers there recently. As soon as the yard has had a chance to cool down, the writers return to it.

The only yard in the city that almost all writers seem to avoid is the 207th Street maintenance yard on the West Side of Manhattan, known to nearly every writer as "the Ghost Yard." The Ghost Yard would seem to be an ideal place to write graffiti since trains of all sorts are stored there in large numbers and the yard is accessible by climbing over a relatively low wall. The writers, however, tend to avoid it. Stories of the origins of the yard's nickname and its bad reputation vary greatly. Caz says that it is inhabited by the ghost of a writer who was killed there one night by yardmen and was "buried beneath the tracks." Kade has gone to the yard with the intention of writing but left when he heard "terrible screams, a dying woman's screams," emanating from the work sheds. Candy's explanation of the yard's name is far less dramatic. She says that the name is derived from the ghostly piles of salt that are stocked there every winter for use in melting ice and that workers there look like ghosts because "they're all white from the salt."

The yards hold many more tangible hazards for writers than ghosts. Trains are frequently moved in the yards, and an unwary writer could be hit by one. Trains stored in lay-ups are hazardous painting sites because in-service trains pass by them closely on either side, and the writer has to climb under the parked train or run to the far side of the tracks to escape being hit. Movement through tunnels is dangerous because the catwalks are high and narrow, it is dark, and there are numerous open grates, abutments, and low-hanging signs and light fixtures that threaten even the slowest-moving writer.

Stories abound of writers who have walked into walls, fallen into pits, been shocked by the third rail, and broken bones when falling on the tracks. Ali, the leader of the Soul Artists group, was severely injured in a tunnel lay-up when a spark from a passing train ignited twenty cans of paint that he had set beside him.

The police believe that the main hazard in the yards and lay-ups is the third rail, which powers the trains and carries a constant current of 650 volts, enough to hurt severely or kill anyone who touches it without being grounded. Most writers are aware of the danger of contact with the third rail but see its hazards as secondary to what they consider the main peril in the yards: the police. Writers will do almost anything to escape a raid: climb under or run along the tops of trains, shimmy down three-story "el" pillars, jump onto moving trains, leap from one station platform to the other, throw themselves onto barbed-wire fences, or run tracks or running boards for miles.

Despite the risks, however, most writers seem to enjoy their forays into the yards. Among those who go to the yards in groups, a sense of shared danger, group effort, and camaraderie usually prevails. Bama has described the pleasure he derived from work in the yards:

> It was fun . . . that's the beauty of the writing. You know, you sit there in the train yard at two o'clock in the morning with four other people and you're spraying and you look down the track and you see all these brothers working on one goal—to make this train beautiful. There's so much peace in that. You got that creative feeling, that vibe that comes out of all that work happening. Everyone's looking out for the man and for workmen and the tenseness, man, it's just a weird feeling. You get close to each other when you're doing this and you've got to trust the next man 'cause if you're not looking, you hope he is.

3

A Brief History of Writing

Henry Chalfant

The writing of graffiti dates back to the wall painting of prehistoric humans. The history of New York City's distinctive form of subway graffiti, however, is generally thought to have begun in the late 1960s when a Washington Heights teenager named Demetrius first started writing his nickname, Taki, and his street number, 183, on walls, stoops, public monuments, and especially in subway stations all over Manhattan.

Early writers—Taki 183, Frank 207, Chew 127, and Julio 204—did not seem to care much what their "hits" (early term for tags) looked like as long as they got them up and people could read them. As hundreds of new writers emerged, however, new emphasis began to be placed on style, on "making your name sing" among all those other names.

At this time some writers sought to make their names stand out by writing them in unusual locations. Soul I, a Manhattan writer, for example, specialized in placing his hits halfway up the sides of large buildings in locations that, according to Tracy 168, "could not be reached by normal humans. It was like he could fly." As writers sought to outdo one another in the placement of hits, great effort was devoted to getting up the first hit in new and unlikely spots. Bama tried to get up the first hit on an upstate New York mountain top:

> I got on a bus one time and went up to Bear Mountain with Moe TR and Iron Mike. We were gonna hit on Bear Mountain. We climbed up that fucker rock up to that Big Moose they got up on the top of the cliff, climbed up on top of the Moose, and went to hit on the belly of the Moose. We hung down over the sides of this thing. It scared the shit out of us 'cause we were 200 feet up and we're hanging there and there's nothing but water below us and rocks and I'm wiping off the dust and what do I see painted under all that dust? Super Kool 223. I was sitting there saying, "You know what we just went through? Wendell did it a little while ago. He's first!" So we had to make ours bigger and better. But just the fact that when I was hanging there and wiped that dust away and under that dust was that Super Kool, that is what I call tagging.

The real competition, however, took place on the trains, and writers began to seek new ways to ensure that their

An outside hit (forerunner of the masterpiece) by Kathy 97.

names would be among the welter of hits that covered the insides. In order to make their names more noticeable, many writers began to embellish them. Kool Jeff turned his "J" into a devil's tail, Lee 163 ran his "E"s together, Wicked Gary surrounded his initials with a box, Cay 161 and Snake 131 put crowns over their names, and Stay High integrated into his signature a stick figure smoking a joint.

The lettering of these hits remained fairly straight and readable, however. Radically different lettering styles began to appear after the arrival in Manhattan of a Philadelphia graffiti writer, Top Cat 126. Top Cat, who claimed to have learned graffiti writing from Philadelphia's legendary Cornbread, wrote his name in long, thin, closely packed letters that stood on little platforms. Top Cat's tags were difficult to read, but that seemed to make them stand out and attract attention all the more, and a number of Manhattan writers took up his style, dubbing it "Broadway Elegant."

Not to be outdone, a number of Brooklyn writers inaugurated a style of their own. Brooklyn-style graffiti was distinguished by the use of free-flowing letters, embellished with hearts, arrows, and swirls. A Bronx style that was basically a combination of the other two also enjoyed a brief period of popularity. Most writers, however, preferred to develop their own personal styles, and the appearance in the early 1970s of large markers gave them a new freedom and ease of movement.

When style alone failed to distinguish individual names from the general welter of tags, writers began to concentrate on development of size and color. Stay High and some others started painting their names on the outsides of the trains in thin white letters that stretched the full length and breadth of a car. Other writers began to silhouette their names with concentric bands of paint or ink in order to create a rainbow effect. In 1972 Super Kool created the first masterpiece (later shortened to "piece").

As tagging styles had changed with the appearance of new tools, so also had an advance in technology, the discovery of the fat cap, led to the creation of the masterpiece. Super Kool had discovered that replacing the narrow-dispersion cap of a spray paint can with the wide-spraying top of a spray foam or spray starch can enabled him to cover large surface areas with broad, smooth sweeps of paint. Armed with a so-altered can of pink paint and a regular can of yellow, Super Kool entered the 221st Street train yard and painted his name in thick pink letters and outlined them with a thin band of yellow. The resulting piece was somewhat sloppy and the letters were irregularly shaped, but it was the most colorful and impressive piece of graffiti that had been done on the subways. It created an immediate sensation with the other writers.

Phase II from the Bronx was the first writer to develop the masterpiece. He started by improving on Super Kool's basic design, writing his name in enormous, puffy, but well-formed and carefully colored and outlined letters that he called bubble letters. Phase had a genius not only for design but for creating names for styles. Within a short time he had developed such variations on his original design as "phasemagorical phantastic" (bubble letters with stars), "bubble cloud" (bubble letters surrounded by a cloud pattern), "checkerboard phase phantastic" (bubble letters crosshatched), "bubble big top" (bubble letters with outsized tops), "squish luscious" (swerving, speed-streaked bubble letters), as well as "stretch bubble," "bubble drip," "spiral-gyro-tasmarific," and dozens of others. Phase set the tone, and other writers began to create and name new bubble letter variations of their own.

The next revolution in style occurred when Pistol I, a Brooklyn writer, painted the first 3-D piece. It consisted of his name painted in red and white and partially outlined with a blue band that gave it a three-dimensional appearance. Fred described the writers' reaction to Pistol's first 3-D: "Writers came from all over the city to see it. It was the talk of the town for a while because everyone wanted to do one but they couldn't conceive of being able to do it. Pistol must have practiced on paper for a long time to get it down. After a while, though, people started to try it, and then everybody was doing it, improving on it, adding touches of their own."

At this point a new term entered graffiti language: style master. Previously titles of honor had been granted to writers only on the basis of the number of pieces or tags they had managed to get up. Now style was also a route to fame and "style wars" began. Some writers even changed their names, hoping that a new combination of letters to write might inspire them to create new designs. Throughout the city writers tried to outdo each other in terms of color and design.

Stan 153 described his battle to hold on to the title of style master in early 1973 and of his personal war with Riff, a competitor:

> Everybody was competing. From one end of the trains to the other there would be beautiful clouds, beautiful colors, beautiful names. This went on for months. Beautiful stuff. But somehow or other I stayed on top as a style master. Then it narrowed down to two basic people, me and Riff, and the war was on. Like, for instance, Riff would change his name to Flip 6, and there'd be beautiful Flip's on the trains and everyone would say, "That's beautiful, what are you going to do about it, Stan?" So just for the spite of it and to keep everybody warmed up I'd change my name to Flik 6, you know, one letter. So Riff would do a Flip and two trains later a Flik would come by. And it would be beautiful and people would say, "Oh wow, who's better?" Then Riff got mad and changed his name to Crunch, and I changed my name to Crack and it went on, and on, and on.

The war went on until they met one night in the number 3 yard and decided to call a truce and work together. They cooperated that night on a "checkerboard cloud-3-D-diamondback Crunch-Crack piece," that, in Stan's words "obliterated the eyeballs." A short time later Stan retired, and Riff went on to new heights.

As pieces improved in technical quality and design, they also began to grow in size. Many writers felt constricted painting below the windows of cars and began to expand their pieces upward into top-to-bottoms and lengthwise into end-to-ends. Aaron 155 has described his reaction to the first top-to-bottom: "Riff revolutionized graffiti with the first top-to-bottom. It was beautiful. It was a half-car wide, yellow 'Riff' with red, bloody drips coming down. And it had cracks painted on it. It took everybody out all over New York, everybody was talking about it. I first saw it when I was on my way to court with my mother, I was jumping up and down on the train, yelling. She didn't understand."

Early bubble letter piece by Phase 2.

Shadow 3-D piece by Jay 00 and a
block-letter 3-D piece by EK.
Lynn Forsdale

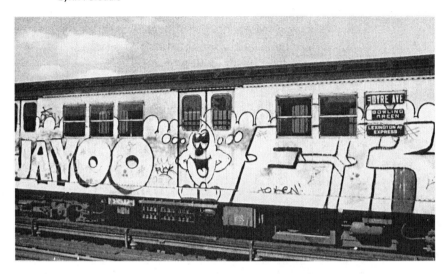

Wild-style 3-D piece by Mitch.
Henry Chalfant

Pieces continued to grow in size and complexity until the first whole car was painted in late 1973. Stan 153 remembers the event:

> Flint 707 came along and outdid the world. He did a three-dimensional piece that took up a whole side of a car, top to bottom and front to back. It was candy-striped, silver and black with a striped blue and white cloud. Since it was 3-D, it looked like it was laying back on the train. At this time, nobody had a thought of doing this sort of piece. You'd have to hang off the train, then you could fall. But he did it and everybody went berserk after that. I was there when he started it. I told him, "You can't do that, there's no way possible." But the next afternoon I noticed all these people, males with their females, kids, standing by the fence looking at the Three Yard, saying, "Wow, look!" I'm walking toward them with Jace and he sees it first. And he just stands there. I said, "What's the matter, what do you see?" And then I looked in the yard and I can't describe the feeling that I got and it was beautiful, it looked like a painting on the side of a train and I understood why other people from all walks of life were standing there looking at it.

As the painting of whole cars grew in popularity, they were enhanced with complex backgrounds and drawings. By the mid-1970s the best writers in the city were specializing in the painting of enormous whole-car murals that often contained caricatures, cartoon characters, outdoor scenes, holiday settings, and even the writers' own interpretations of life in the city. Eventually some writers came to find even whole cars too constricting and started painting two-car "worms." Lee was one of them:

> The best piece I ever done to my mind was the "Earth Is Hell—Heaven Is Life" two-car. "Heaven Is Life" had clear letters and soft colors. It was my view of heaven. Flowers and mountains, the sun, a dove, butterflies, and God in a preaching attitude with his hands up. On the next car, I went off. I told the city how it really looks. There was a soldier holding a gun, his whole body was Shadow Green, and near him it said "Stop the War." I drew factories that were gray and dim with smokestacks. I drew a man hang-

ing his dog, to emphasize cruelty to animals. I drew a dude choking his lady. I drew blood splats and I drew the President up there preaching, with people looking up to him. Behind him was an American flag, but it wasn't really, and it said "Vote for me and I'll give you what you want." And "Vote for Nixon," and all that. It had missiles laid up, the sky was very dim, shaded with orange from fires. And it said "Earth Is Hell" in burning letters. And the whole car looked black. If I ever do it again, I'll do even more. I'll do five whole cars of the good, five whole cars of the bad, with angels blowing horns and God detailed to the death!

At about the same time that whole cars started appearing, another new and different form became popular: throw-ups. Until that time the term throw-up had been used to describe pieces that were badly colored, sloppy, and poorly conceived. It took a writer like IN to embrace those qualities and find a way to turn them into an asset.

In the summer of 1975, according to many writers, IN decided to bring the spirit of competition purely on the basis of getting up (sheer numbers of pieces) that had long dominated writing on the insides to writing on the outsides of the trains. He chose his name because it was short and easy to form and he did not have to use much paint to write it. He then began to practice, painting his name in a messy, uneven version of bubble letters. At first he painted only his name once or twice on each car he encountered, but then he started "bombing" the trains, covering whole cars with what he referred to as "my throw-ups."

At first other writers looked down on IN for his lack of style, but as his completed throw-ups began to number in the thousands, they had to admit that, style or no style, he sure was getting up. As IN's fame grew, other writers began adopting two-letter names and doing throw-ups of their own. Even Jester, one of the most revered stylists of the day, changed his name to DY and began painting solely throw-ups. Other writers switched back and forth between throw-up names and piecing names, throw-ups to get their names around and pieces to show style.

Whole-car painters like Lee and Blade openly denounced throw-ups as "a lot of jalopy" and began lamenting the grow-

Remnants of IN's "#5,000 Celebration
Whole Car." Gabriella Oldham

Pieces by Blade and Ammo.
Lynn Forsdale

Cartoon rat by CYA.

ing popularity of throw-ups as "the death of graffiti." IN celebrated the completion of his five thousandth throw-up by painting a spectacular star-covered, rainbow-striped whole car, as if to prove that he could do a burner if he wanted to. He then resumed painting the same pale, runny throw-ups as before and carried on, it is said, until he completed ten thousand of them. At that point, according to Tracy 168, "IN was declared King of Everything." STAN 153 confirmed this, stating, "He got what he wanted, he was king of it all. Ten thousand pieces! They were not beautiful, they were not pretty, but he got up!" After painting an "IN #10,000 Celebration 3-D Whole-Car," IN retired. Since that time, throw-ups have remained popular though they do not dominate the trains as they once did. Whole cars, top-to-bottoms, end-to-ends, and pieces continue to be painted.

Writers continue to develop new styles and new techniques. Recent innovations include the development of color blending (also called fading), a complicated spray-painting process in which colors are made to appear to fade into one another, moving gradually from lighter to darker shades of paint. New lettering styles include "computer," "mechanical," and "gothic." New variations on old styles have emerged as well, including "soft crash" (overlapping bubble letters) and "shadow 3-D," which uses whole families of colors and results in a three-dimensional effect so realistic that, in Dea-2's words, "It looks like you could pull it right off the train."

Subway writing in all forms continues to appear in New York. Contrary to claims by former transit police chief Garelik that "the fad is dying out," there seem to be as many names around as ever. The MTA increased its normal maintenance of trains in celebration of the authority's diamond jubilee in 1980 and the trains were cleaned at a furious rate. The writers nonetheless got their names back up about as fast as the scrubbers could take them off.

The future of writing on the outsides of trains is uncertain at this time, though not because of the washing of the trains. A number of paint manufacturers have redesigned the tops of their spray cans in such a way that fat caps can no longer be fitted to them. The disappearance of fat-capped paint cans could, in Caz's words, "Send graffiti backwards, back to what it was with skinny caps all the way." Fred, however, has faith that the problem can be overcome and has stated that "the writers will find another way. Technology plays a heavy part in graffiti. It would be hard to do throw-ups or pieces or anything but tags with a skinny cap. But then styles will change and new styles will be made up to suit the materials. . . . Wait and see. . . . The whole thing will develop all over again."

4

Writers

Lynn Forsdale

When asked, "What sorts of kids write graffiti?" police officer Kevin Hickey of the New York Transit Police Department's graffiti squad replied, "The type of kids that live in New York City. They range from the ultra-rich to the ultra-poor. There is no general classification of the kids; it's just that a typical New York City kid will write graffiti, if given the opportunity and if this is what his friends do." Another police officer, Conrad Lesnewski, agreed: "Also some of the kids apprehended— their fathers were professors at Columbia, NYU, some were CPAs, some were doctors, architects. They live in a thousand-dollar house, apartments, some are living in a $1.98-a-month ghetto. There's no generalizations."

Writers come from every race, nationality, and economic group in New York City. One graffiti organization, the Nation of Graffiti Artists (NOGA), has members representing numerous ethnic groups, including Chinese-Americans, West Indians, Ukrainians, Filipinos, Dominicans, and Nigerians. In economic background members range from the sons and daughters of the wealthy to kids who live in the streets. Most NOGA members, and possibly most writers, are poor blacks, Hispanics, and whites. Although there are no data available on the ethnic and economic backgrounds of writers, it appears that Tracy 168 is correct in his contention that "you got hundreds of different kinds of writers out there."

Most writers are young. According to police records and many writers, most young people begin their writing careers at about eleven years of age and retire from writing at age sixteen. On the subject of age, Hickey has said, "These kids start writing when they're about ten years old and they'll work graffiti from ten, eleven, twelve, thirteen, fourteen, and fifteen. The majority of them will stop graffiti by their sixteenth birthday because they realize that once they turn sixteen they're not kids anymore. They'll be treated as adults and whether they're given a severe penalty in court or not, they will be fingerprinted and photographed as a criminal and they will retain this record for the rest of their lives."

There are exceptions to these age limits. Some writers are said to have begun writing at age nine or younger, and others, often after a brief initial retirement at sixteen, return to writing for comebacks that can take them into their twenties.

Lesnewski notes, "We have kids now nineteen, twenty, twenty-one years old, still painting graffiti. One comes down with his baby in his arms, with his wife, and is still out painting graffiti." Among the writers whom police files identify as over the age of eighteen and still active are Butch 2 (twenty years old), Slave (twenty-one), Kindo (twenty-two), Wasp (twenty-three), and Blade (twenty-four). The average age of most writers, however, seems to be fourteen or fifteen. According to former transit police chief Sanford Garelik, "More than 70 percent of the juveniles arrested for graffiti have been fifteen year olds."

Although males predominate as writers, there are a number of well-known female writers, and many graffiti groups include active female members. Among the best known have been Barbara 62, Eva 62, Charmin, Stoney, Grape I 897, TNT Toni, and Swan. Charmin won fame among the writers as the first person to tag the Statue of Liberty. Barbara and Eva 62 (they usually wrote together and their names are usually mentioned in combined form) achieved a great tagging feat while on a trip to Miami. As Bama tells the story:

> My mother came back from Florida, she had a picture she took in front of Jackie Gleason's studio. On the wall in back of my mother, it said "Barbara and Eva 62—Hello New York!" She showed me that picture and I freaked out. Wendell came back from South Carolina. He told me he knew what Barbara and Eva did. They took a bus down to Florida and everywhere the bus stopped, he said he saw their names. In every place the bus stopped in, they hit all the way down the East Coast. At all those little Howard Johnsons. Everywhere.

Bama has also told of a historic joint effort by Charmin and *Barbara and Eva 62:*

> DeWitt Clinton [High School, in the Bronx]. The boy's locker room. The downstairs bathroom next to the showers. "Barbara and Eva 62," "Charmin." Spray paint. In the bathroom downstairs by the shower! I didn't go to the school, they didn't go to the school. I had trouble getting in there. These are girls and there isn't any way a girl

can get through the door at Clinton because Clinton is an all-boy school. And yet they were downstairs and it was their handwriting.

In 1973 Charmin and Stoney, a writer who had been a member of the Brooklyn Ex-Vandals "graffiti gang," were invited to join the United Graffiti Artists organization (UGA), an elite gathering of the city's most prominent writers. This can be seen as an indication that they were widely considered to be among the most highly skilled writers of their time.

Today there appear to be fewer well-known female writers than in the past. Carmen was a member of the Funkadelics, a writing group based at the High School of Art and Design in Manhattan, but she was not allowed to go with the male members of the group to write at the train yards. Her friend Son One said, "Some of the guys . . . they want graffiti to stick to the guys." Apparently many male writers agree with Rat: "We don't bring girls to the yards 'cause if they get hurt we'll feel responsible." Carmen later left the Funkadelics and attempted to start an all-girl group but could not recruit any members.

Many female writers appear to avoid the yards by choice, preferring to limit their efforts to train tagging and painting on the walls of buildings. Kathy 161, however, has been known to go to the yards, as have Luz and China.

There are a number of traits that most writers have in common. Primary among these is an interest in the lore, language, and techniques of graffiti writing. Writers enjoy talking about writing, both among themselves and to outsiders, and take delight in using the jargon that they have created.

Writers in general are not humble. They tend toward exaggeration when talking of their own abilities and status in the graffiti world, particularly when talking to outsiders or lesser writers. A notable exception to this tendency is the behavior of famous writers, who generally exhibit the sort of quiet dignity that is considered appropriate to those of high position.

Because slow-moving writers tend to get caught by subway conductors or the police, most writers are fast runners. And most possess the physical ability necessary for climbing high fences, vaulting subway turnstiles, or shimmying down el pillars. There are exceptions. OZ, a chubby and slow-moving fifteen-year-old writer, compensated for his lack of speed by wearing a dark blue MTA-regulation-style raincoat and carrying his paint in an attache case whenever he went to the yards. According to Blood Tea, "When a raid came down OZ would just walk away, slowly. Nobody ever stopped him."

Almost invariably writers have good handwriting, an important quality much appreciated by teachers. Elaine Spielberg of the High School of Art and Design calls their handwriting "beautiful." "They can't always spell, but their assignments, when they do them, are a pleasure to look at."

Writers frequently have an interest in art. Many develop skills in drawing through their work in the black books, and writers frequently express a desire to go on to careers as cartoonists or animators. They take a greater interest in techniques of illustration, photography, calligraphy, printing, and painting than many other people their age. Writers sometimes are interested in art history, seeking inspiration for new designs for their pieces in art books and museums. In the case of Lee and Fred, such study resulted in a strong feeling of identification with artists of the past. Lee has said:

> I was reading this fat history of art book. I was reading about how the cave men were so advanced that when they drew animals to show their children how to hunt and to show their type of culture, they knew they couldn't do them in the front of the cave but went to the deepest depths of the cave where they had to crawl. And they'd do it where it would stay forever. And it was like us. Like we go into the tunnels and we'd go all the way to the deepest parts to find the trains and maybe you leave a signature on the wall and it stays there for years. And when you go into the tunnels you say, "Wow, look at that Cliff, look at that IN, look at that Phase." You go into some of those lay-ups. You see a lot of big Cliff pieces and old pieces back there. I look at those pieces and it's like serious.

Fred also feels a strong identification with writers of the past, in his case, the early Christians of Rome: "Like the early Christians in Rome were forced to go down into the catacombs and they painted beautiful images of Christ. . . . They. . . were forbidden to depict Christ. . . . It was against the law, it was the death penalty, but those people went on. They were down!"

Although many writers talk of pursuing a career in art, only a few actually attend art school, and fewer still manage to make a living as artists. One notable example is Bama, who attended the Pratt Institute in New York and today is an animator for a company that makes television commercials.

A number of writers have started art-related businesses. Tracy 168 paints graffiti-style signs for stores; Lee, Slave, Spin, and Caz recently were paid $1,500 to paint murals in the interior of the Unique Clothing Warehouse store in Greenwich Village; and many others earn money by painting designs and names on jackets and jeans for other young people.

Although most writers prefer doing their work exclusively on the sides of trains, a number also paint on canvas and seek recognition as serious artists. Many writers who have joined NOGA and other graffiti organizations now paint on canvas not only with spray paint and markers but with oils and acrylics.

Many graffiti writers believe that they are beautifying the city with their train painting and consider their writing a public service. Police officer Lesnewski has quoted one captured writer as saying, "You can cut both my hands, you can cut both my arms off, I'll still paint the trains every day because I owe it to the people of New York City to make these trains beautiful."

Although they have much in common with other city kids, graffiti writers as a community are more remarkable for their differences. In a much-fragmented city, writers are among the few young people to reach beyond the bounds of their own neighborhoods and travel throughout the city, meeting and getting to know young people from other boroughs and a variety of ethnic and economic groups.

Names

The names that writers mark and paint on trains are usually not those on their birth certificates. There are exceptions: Mark's real name is Mark, Tracy 168's is Tracy, Julio 204's is Julio. More often, however, a writing name is a nickname or street name that the writer is given, a variation on the writer's real name, or a name that the writer devises himself.

Bama has discussed the sources of the writing names of a number of his contemporaries:

> Basically they were names that meant something to them. . . . Tabu, he liked the name Tabu, like it meant danger. You know, "Look out for Tabu; he's taboo." Turban liked the term *turban*. There was a gang called the Turbans. We thought he was part of that but he wasn't; he just liked the name. Sweet Duke, his nickname was Duke and he thought he was sweet. Phase II was a step beyond the first phase, and he wasn't the third phase. He was the second, between the first and the third, so that's where Phase got his name from. . . . Lee, his name was Lee. So that was easy for him. Super Kool, that wasn't a problem. He knew what he was. He said "I'm super cool." Kool Kevin was Kool Kevin because Kevin was cool. Kool Jeff was Kool Jeff because Jeff was cool. And they came after the main Kool, Super Kool who was like the father of the Kools in the Bronx. So you had all these Kools. And then you had the unique names, like Ray B. No problem there, Raymond B———. Charmin, well, we guess her name came from Charmin. She liked the name Charmin. Barbara 62, she lived on 62d Street and her name was Barbara. Eva 62, she lived on 62d Street and her name was Eva. Stoney, she picked that name but I guess she would have to answer that, why she used Stoney. She's so soft and beautiful and she's using a hard name like Stoney. . . . Moe TR, Michael of Edenwald. There's no problem there, he was Michael, he lived in Edenwald [Projects] and he was the 'Riter. The Train 'Riter. Iron Mike was short but he had a heart of iron. . . . Stay High picked his name because that was something that he did; he stayed high. . . . Like most of the names were a part of the character. They related to something within that person. Hulk 62. Hulk was a big motherfucker. . . . Cool Herc? He was the size of Hercules. Cat 2233. Everyone called him Cat because he usually used to sneak around a lot. He was a second-story man. He liked to rob places so they called him the Cat and he lived on 223d Street in the second building. 2-223. That's how you'd find him. And that's basically how guys and girls pick their names. Usually it has something to do with their

*Pieces by Cuda (whose writing name is
a shortened version of barracuda) and
Mark (whose real name is Mark).*
Henry Chalfant

personality, their being. You know, it was related to their street name, everybody had a street name. Usually your street name was something that picked out your personality. So that's how we got our names.

When they first start writing graffiti, writers will often run through a number of different names before they hit upon one that they like. Bama called himself Ka-Tel and King Ding before settling on the names Bama and Amrl, which he used alternately; Keno started out writing Nitro and Sex Machine; Rat changed his name from Mouse. Stan 153 has described the process of selecting his name:

> In 1970 I became a graffiti artist because of my best friend. His name was David. He started writing Dave I, right? So I said, "Hey, well, let me try a name." So then I started out with the name Blue Flame and it just didn't hit it off. People said, "Blue Flame, ha-ha-ha." And that made me feel kind of funny. I tried a few other names then like Cool Stanley, Stanley P, Stanley Doo-Wah. Didn't quite work. So I ran into another graffiti artist who's a friend of mine from the first grade, Cliff 159 and another one whose name was . . . Jester 1. They said, "Stop writing all that and try your real name." So I said, "O.K., Stanley." And they said, "No, it doesn't sound right. Try Stan." So I put it together with my street number 153.

When a writer chooses a name, a great deal of emphasis is placed on picking a name that "pieces good." A writer who does not feel comfortable with the name or has difficulty finding a style in which to write it will change it. Long names are unpopular because writing them takes too much time. According to Son One, "If you pick a long name, it's not going to work out. Usually the limit's five letters."

Names are derived from many sources. Bama says that his name is "an East African word meaning 'poet' or 'prophet'"; Adom 2 got his name from science class (a misspelling of *atom*); Mitch (whose real name is Mitch) got his secondary names, Tue and 7-Up, from the abbreviation for Tuesday on the calendar and his favorite soft drink. Keno's name is a misspelling of the name of a character in John Steinbeck's *The Pearl*. Keno explained how he found it: "I was just passing through the book because I had to write it as a book report and I just saw Keno. And I said, 'Dag, it's a nice four-letter word,' so I messed around and wrote around with it and I just got hooked into the name."

Hispanic writers frequently choose Spanish or "Spanglish" words for names. For example, Mico's name is Dominican slang for "monkey"; Mono's name also means "monkey"; Chino Malo's name, in his own words, means "bad Chink"; Papo's name means "Dad"; and Veza's name is short for *cerveza*, meaning "beer."

Writers sometimes choose names that are variations on those of other writers. Slick apparently was inspired in his choice of a name by such well-known earlier writers as Super Slick and Slick-1. It is considered a serious offense for a writer to borrow another's name wholly, but he is permitted to use the same name if a differentiating number is placed after it. Adom 2, for example, originally wrote Adom and added the "2" only after an earlier holder of the name threatened to "kick his ass" for "name-biting."

Roman numerals frequently are used to differentiate between writers with the same basic name. These numbers, however, are often not employed in strict order. For example, Phase II preceded Phase I, who was followed by Phase IV and then Phase III.

The longer numbers that follow many writers' names have a variety of meanings. Taki 183 and Lee 163 used their street numbers. Later, perhaps because they did not wish to give any aid to police officers who might be trying to track them, writers generally abandoned this practice and chose numbers with other meanings (Bot 007, is a James Bond fan) or with a pleasing sound (Pel 888, and Sep 2121 are examples).

Writers frequently use more than one name, switching between them when they tire of one, when they develop a style that is suited only to one of them, or when they write one so often that it has become "hot" (the police are looking for the holder of the name). Writers also frequently have long names that they use when painting large pieces, and shorter, usually two-letter, names for use in throw-ups.

To some writers their writing names are symbols of a life far different from that which they experience at home or at school. A young person who seems unexceptional in most contexts may be a highly regarded "king" or "master outlaw" in the writing world. To such writers their names take on a special importance, for it is by these self-chosen names that they are known to the people from whom they would most like to win respect and admiration, and it is by the writing of these names that they hope to achieve success. Wicked Gary is typical of writers who feel that a sense of identity and pride can be derived from writing one's name: "A lot of people found . . . security and comfort in dealing with their name. It was strengthening who they were to themselves. . . . Writing your name identifies who you are. The more you write your name, the more you begin to think about and the more you begin to be about who you are. Once you start doing that, you start to assert your individualism and when you do that, you have an identity."

Toys

The word *toy* is used by writers to refer to anything insignificant. Small pens are called "toy markers"; short-run trains, like the Times Square–Grand Central shuttle, are "toy trains"; and, especially, *toys* is used to describe inferior or inexperienced writers. Bama defined the term in this way: "At first a toy was someone . . . it was anything that wasn't real. Like a guard was a 'toy cop.' Someone who was writing on trains and wasn't real we called a toy. That was a person who was doing marker hits or spray hits but just couldn't hang, didn't have nothing happening with his name, his style, his color, his design, anything." Keno's definition is similar: "A toy is someone who doesn't get up and has a different style. . . . As they say in my language (I've got a lot of slang words) they've got a lot of 'wacky' style. Toys have got a wacky way of writing. In other words, they can't write."

Style is given important consideration in determining whether a writer is a toy, and a writer who lacks the talent or experience to use markers or spray paint effectively is often denounced as such. The term is also used in reference to writers who are judged to be lacking in nerve or cool and to refer to writers who are police informers. The most important criterion by which toy status is determined is whether a writer has managed to get up.

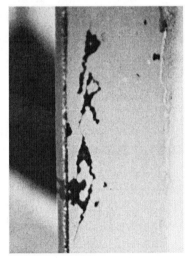

KR (whose throw-up is barely visible) is denounced as a "toy."

The mark of Pray, the "king of the city."

Adom 2, who only recently started writing, has talked about toys and the effort that is required of him if he is to avoid being considered one: "A toy is somebody who doesn't do so well, somebody who has a name but doesn't get up. My friend told me that I don't need to be no toy, 'cause I can get some paint and some magic markers and go out and tag all one day and get my name up a lot and then I won't be no toy."

Regardless of his style, a writer who gets up a great deal is rarely called a toy. Beginners are at a disadvantage in this regard because they have to bear the label of toy or "DGA" ("Don't Get Around") until they have proved themselves through long hours of work in the yards. Chino Malo, a highly experienced writer, prefers to avoid using toy altogether and looks at the whole matter philosophically: "I don't believe in toys, because a toy is a beginner and everybody starts out as a beginner. . . . I wouldn't say it insults you. It wouldn't insult me if they called me a toy because I know what I am and what I stand for. Now if they called my friend, like my friend who just started tagging last week, a toy, . . . I'd say, don't get mad, it's true, you're just a beginner, right?"

The term *toy* is also used occasionally to refer to a writer who has experience but is sorely lacking in other qualities. As Bama has said, "If you were stupid, even if you had something with your style . . . you were considered a toy because you were acting like a toy." The writers most generally thought of in this way are those who cause trouble for other writers by making too much noise in the yards, by smashing windows or otherwise damaging trains, by harassing or stealing from passengers at subway stations, and, especially by informing on other writers. Use of the word *toy* in reference to an experienced writer is considered to be a powerful denunciation, and it is used in face-to-face confrontations with experienced writers only in anticipation of an argument or a fight.

Fame

At the opposite end of the spectrum from toys are writers who "have fame." Writers, like their graffiti, travel throughout the city, and the names of famous writers are often known by writers in all five boroughs. Since most writers share a desire for widespread renown, fame is considered the ultimate in graffiti-writing achievement.

Fame can be won in a number of different ways. The fastest way is to win instant fame, which comes to any writer lucky enough to have his work immortalized in the media. Writers constantly scan newspapers, hoping to find a photograph of a subway train in which one of their pieces "comes out." Derailments, surges in subway crime, and occasional subway rides taken by the mayor and other city officials are all events that can yield photographs that can bring fame to many writers. Writers whose work appears in the newspapers keep the clippings in scrapbooks or carry them with them to show to other writers.

Television can also bring fame, though few writers can hope to match the achievement of P-Nut 2, Jester, and Diablo whose works appeared briefly in the introduction to *Welcome Back Kotter*. As Keno has said, "They say, 'Look at my name!' . . . It's like they've got their own TV show."

Films shot in New York City can bring fame to writers. When "the [subway] lines come out" in a movie, the writers head for the theaters in droves. Dean won fame when one of his tags showed up in *Saturday Night Fever*, and Bama has provided other examples:

> . . . like Super Kool was in the *Exorcist*. That train that pulls into the station when the priest was coming to visit his mother? Big Super Kool . . . and *Death Wish*, especially *Death Wish*, 'cause that was Central Park. Jester and all the Broadway Boys had a field day in that movie. Cliff and a lot of cats got play in *Death Wish*, especially with scenes in the trains. . . . They had a pilot film for Channel 2 with Telly Savalas playing a murderer who was chasing this chick. Where did she run? He chased her into a yard. The New Lots yard. Graffiti for days.

The desire for instant fame has led many writers to make special efforts to try to get their work into the media. Detective sergeant Morris Bitchachi of the Transit Police Department's graffiti squad has given an example:

> We wanted to interview eight or ten kids that were graffiti writers. We had a reporter come down here, so we put the word out that we wanted seven to eight kids. We put the word out to twelve kids. That day how many kids showed

**Dust declares himself "king" of the #6
line.** Ted Pearlman

**PB 5 claims to be "King of the A's"
(the IND A line).** Ted Pearlman

up, about a hundred? We had to take them out to the park and play ball with them because the word got out that a reporter's gonna interview them. . . . After they were interviewed, they kept calling up every day, "When is that article coming out?"

Although writers prize instant fame, it is not as significant as the fame that can be won through diligence and hard work. The fame most honored by writers is won through getting up. Chino Malo has said, "The more you get up, the more famous you are." Estimates of the amount of writing necessary for winning fame vary from writer to writer. Candy says, "You do pieces every day and you get more than two hundred pieces, then you got fame." Most writers set the figure much higher.

A writer who has managed to get up more than anyone else on a particular line is declared king of the line. When a writer wins such a title, the name is spread among all writers, and he is considered to have won fame of the highest sort. Most subway lines have two kings at any given time. One, a king of the insides, is the writer who has managed to tag his name more than anyone else on the insides of the trains. The king of the outsides is the writer, usually a throw-up artist, whose name appears most frequently on the outsides of the trains.

Because trains are periodically scrubbed by the MTA and new pieces and tags appear constantly, these titles frequently change hands. Determinations as to which writers should be granted these titles are made by the writers through informal votes, arguments, and occasional tag- or piece-counting sessions in stations and yards around the city.

Style can play a part in the winning of fame. Writers who paint particularly impressive pieces or whole cars and get up enough to be seen widely can win reputations among the writers. Occasionally writers so distinguish themselves in style and prolificity that they are declared kings of style (the terms *star* and *style master* are also used occasionally). In order to become a king of style, a writer must get up a great deal and with style. The majority of such writers' pieces must be accounted burners, and their spray-painting technique and sense of design must be of the highest order. Lee of the Fabulous Five is widely considered by writers to be a king of style, and there appear to be few others. Apparently the title is rarely granted.

The most famous writer in New York today, to whom some writers refer as king of the city, is a person who cares nothing for style and uses only a ballpoint pen or a drill bit to mark trains, walls, and telephone booths. This person, known to the writers as Pray, has, according to the *New York Post*, "scratched the words 'Pray' and 'Worship God' onto almost all of the New York Telephone Company's public phones."[1] The identity of Pray is a subject writers frequently discuss. Fred has claimed that Pray is an old man, "a wino who lives in a doorway down on Eighth Street." Tracy 168 believes that Pray is a nurse who "used to work in the psychiatric ward at Bellevue but turned Jesus Freak and went insane." One of the few writers who actually claims to have met Pray is Bama. In a recent interview Bama and Wicked Gary talked about Pray:

Bama:

. . . an eighty-year-old lady. A white lady. A very inverted person. I don't know what her story is in terms of what makes her write "Pray" and "Jesus Saves," but . . .

Gary:

She's freaked out.

Bama:

But that woman has hit every phone booth in this city. Neighborhoods that no white lady shouldn't ever even be *seen* in, this wench has been in. Every train station on every subway map you'll see her name. . . . To this day you can go into any telephone booth in this city and look on the change box and you will see "Jesus Saves" or "Pray." The lady was fantastic. I met her on Flatbush Avenue when I was working at the Record Rack. She came into the store, not into the store, but into the lobby and scraped her name . . . proceeded to go across the street into the Chinese restaurant and scrape her name into two phone booths and came back across the street and scraped her name on the eye doctor, then the drug store, then the fabric store on the corner. When she got to the fabric store I realized who she was and approached her and she's a very inverted person and very afraid and she kind of freaked out so I really didn't get a chance to talk to her. . . .

Interviewer:

Is she respected?

Bama:

Oh, yeah. Shit, anybody who hit every phone booth in this city gots to be respected!

Gary:

A lot of them don't even know she's female. All they see is the "Pray," but the word is that "Pray gets up!" Pray is bad!

Bama:

. . . she looks like a bag lady . . . a little tiny old drawn-up lady who hangs in corners, scraping things on things. . . . She could do it in front of cops because no one looks at an old lady, no one, so she's got total freedom. I know she's never got busted. Nobody's gonna mess with her.

Socializing

Interviewer:

Do graffiti writers know each other?

Keno:

It's like a family.

Chino Malo:

I know guys from Brooklyn, I know guys from the Bronx, I know guys from all over. I've known guys to mention my name when I'm beside them and I don't even know them.

When writers meet for the first time they invariably greet each other with the words, "What do you write?" In order to identify a writer among the general subway crowds, one only has to look for a young person who stares intently at every train that passes through a station. Police officer Theodore Rotun has said, "That's the way an officer picks them up right away. . . . You'll see them watch the trains, it's like they don't want to, but . . . he's gotta watch the train. Once you see the eyes move, then you know that this kid's hooked on this; you know that either he's hooked as an admirer or a doer. You know."

Writers are usually interested in meeting other writers and when they spot someone, albeit a stranger, who looks as if he might be a fellow writer, often they will introduce themselves. Bama has described the process of identifying writers on the trains:

> You'd check a guy out on a train and you'd say, this guy looks like a writer, I wonder who he is. So you do something like take your finger and mimic writing on the wall and see if the guy noticed it. And he'd look at it and probably acknowledge it in some strange way, like he'd pull out a marker and put it back. That's when you'd get up and go over and say, "What do you write, man?" . . . I could tell a writer. Writers always looked strange in trains 'cause they're looking around trying to find out who's who in the car so they can hit.

Once writers have greeted each other, their next concern is to determine each other's status. If both are famous names, they will often greet each other effusively, praising each other's work and often proposing a mutual writing venture for a future date. If they are carrying black books, they exchange autographs.

Lesser writers treat each other in a similar manner when they meet, though if one considers himself more experienced than the other an argument may ensue as to which one is more of a toy. A lesser writer who meets a famous writer usually will show the latter great respect and may request an autograph for his black book. If the well-known writer takes a liking to his less-famous peer, he may extend to him an invitation to hang around with him and may offer to take him along to the yards one night. Such invitations are highly prized, and toys usually take advantage of such opportunities to get hooked up with famous writers.

In the early days of subway writing, writers tended to work on their own, and only those who went to school together or lived near each other ever got together. By 1972, however, writers had begun to gather at a number of writers' corners around the city. The first writers' corner was located at 188th Street and Audubon Avenue in Manhattan and was presided over by Stitch I. Former UGA director Hugo Martinez has described this meeting place: "Here the best writers of

Manhattan, the Bronx and Brooklyn would come to meet, sign in, exchange gossip and, if the feelings were right, go out and hit together. Here also toy writers could look upon their heroes and perhaps get their autographs. (Only the best writers of Manhattan were allowed to consider themselves privileged to add "W.C. 188" to their signatures.)"[2]

Many of the most famous Bronx writers of the early 1970s met at the Coffee Shop, a doughnut shop across the street from DeWitt Clinton High School. After meeting and greeting each other, this group would usually head down to the Concourse, the subway station at 149th Street and Grand Concourse in the Bronx. Its lower platform is an ideal spot from which to watch the trains because it is a point of convergence for the 2, 4, and 5 lines of the IRT. Here the Coffee Shop writers would join numerous other writers, who also spent time at this important writers' corner. When Stan 153 first tried to win acceptance at the Coffee Shop and the Concourse,

> Tie 174 said to me, "Listen, let's go up to the Coffee Shop." I didn't know what it was, but he said "Come up with me and I'll introduce you to some people." So we went up to DeWitt Clinton High School and there's a coffee shop on, I think, Mosholu Parkway, and I walked in and I saw all these guys all over the place and I said, "Wow, look at all these people, who are they?"
>
> There was a tough guy with a scar across his face; we called him Zipper Lip. He used to write Pearl 149. He walked up and said, "Whatchu write?" I said, "Stan 153." So he said "Stan who?" And I said "Stan 153." "DGA!" He yelled it out across the coffee shop, and everybody immediately focused their attention on me. I was like, "Who, me? I'm an artist too." But at that time I wasn't an artist. I was just a little toy, a DGA.
>
> Then I met T-Rex 131 which was a guy that was about six foot five, which made me feel like a shrimp. I said, "You're the great T-Rex, right?" And he said, "Yes, I'm the great T-Rex." And I said, "Please, Mister, would you sign my book?" And he said, "Shuurre." And this giant hand came down and picked it up and gave me an original T-Rex. And it went on for two or three hours, signing books, and then Tie said, "Come on, it's time to leave." And I said,

"Where are we going now?" "To the Concourse." So I said, "Concourse?" because I was from Manhattan and didn't know too much about the Bronx. So I went to the Concourse and I went through the great humiliation again of "What's your name." "Oh, I'm Stan 153." "Who? DGA!" When a train came in they said, "Your name on that train?" And I said, "No, my name ain't on this line." And they said, "What line is your name on, the number Z?" And I said, "No, it's on the 3s." And they said, "O.K., we're going to the 3 line. If your name's there, you can hang out. If it isn't, 'bye guy.'" So we went to 96th Street and Broadway. It was me, Topcat 126, El Marko, Bug 170, Phase II. I didn't know Phase II then; he was just a guy everybody seemed to idolize. So we're at 96th Street and after a half an hour of waiting, my name came up. "Is that your name?" It was an ugly piece of gook on the side of the train, but I said, "That's my name! That's my name!" "O.K. You can hang out."

When they said that, I said to myself, "I'm accepted. The Bronx people accept me!" So I started hanging out in the Bronx. Every day it was the Coffee Shop or the Concourse. And after about four, five months I had met a lot of graffiti artists. I met such greats as Jet Star, Junior 161, Cay 161, Joe 182, all the originals, the ones who really originated New York graffiti.

As word spread of the gatherings at the Concourse, writers began to travel there from all over the city. Wicked Gary, a Brooklyn writer, has spoken of his journeys to the Concourse:

We started to venture out into Manhattan and the Bronx to try to find these people, to let them know our ideas and get involved with them. Once we found out the Bronx had a hangout at 149th Street and Grand Concourse we started going up in groups, finding out who was who and what was what . . . and we started growing, 'cause we had our own communication system. If you needed to know anything that happened on the subway, you could ask a graffiti artist and he could tell you. . . . We knew everything that was happening. That was our playground, that was our work and . . . we were involved. Schedules of trains, schedules of tunnels, we had information on everything. It was a whole other system of communication and interaction from the normal system that we deal with like the English language and money and stuff like that. We had our own language, our own technology, terminology. The words we had meant things to us that nobody else could identify. We had our own tools of the trade. We had all this happening for us.

Soon writers' corners were established at the Brooklyn Bridge subway station in Manhattan (intersection of the 4, 5, and 6 lines of the IRT), and at Atlantic Avenue in Brooklyn (the 2, 3, 4, and 5 lines of the IRT and the D, QB, and M as well). Writers then began to travel from one writers' corner to another, introducing themselves to each other and picking up news from a growing writers' grapevine. Bama has described this growing network of communication:

> Meeting was fun. Like going into a place like Brooklyn and just riding around and you'd see this cat and you'd say, "What do you write?" He'd say, "Wicked Gary," and you'd say, "Wicked Gary who writes for the Ex-Vandals?" "Oh, you know about me?" "Hey, I'm Bama, AMRL." "Oh yeah, from the Bronx." And someone from Brooklyn who knows about you, and you knowing about somebody from another borough is a beautiful thing. The communication was tight. It got to the point where you could say something at Atlantic Avenue, and an hour later at 149th Street and Grand Concourse, you'd hear it over.

The writers' corners flourished for a number of years, and new generations of writers continued to congregate at the Concourse, Atlantic Avenue, and Brooklyn Bridge, as the earlier writers had. However, pressure on the police from city officials to put a stop to graffiti writing led to a crackdown on the writers' gathering places. Police officer Theodore Rotun has explained the Transit Police Department's strategy in regard to the writers' corners: "A graffiti artist is like a pyromaniac who starts a fire; he has to stay around and watch it. If his graffiti can't go from one end of the city to another and he can't brag and sit at his writers' corners . . . then it's no good. . . . When they congregate too much, like in the daytime, the cops will take them in, so when that place gets hot they move on."

Writers' Corner 149.

Today when writers go to the corners, they try to keep a low profile, seeking to avoid the attention of the police. In order to keep a corner from becoming hot, the writers shun those of their peers who tend to attract police interest. Police officer Conrad Lesnewski explains, "They have a tendency of policing their own. If they're at a certain locale, just sitting and waiting for the trains to come by, and a friend of theirs comes by who is known to be a bad guy, a bagsnatcher, or a mugger, or something like that, they will tell him, 'get lost, we don't want you around. Because when you're around here, you bring the heat down, you bring trouble for us.' They know their bounds. They know they can go so far without going beyond that."

Because of the police crackdown on the corners, communication among writers from different neighborhoods and boroughs is not as tight today as it once was. Writers now socialize mainly with those other writers whom they meet in school or on the street or with fellow members of various writing groups. They seem to derive some feeling of closeness from watching each other's names pass by on the trains, though they may not know those who wrote them personally. Certain writers' reputations as well as various items of gossip seem to be generally known by writers throughout the city, but news does not travel as fast or as accurately as it once did.

Although today's writers do seem, generally, to be aware of the history of the writers' corners, they rarely spend time at them. Daze, a young writer, said of the current state of the corners:

> The writers' corner, at 149th. That's where the writers used to hang out. But nobody goes there anymore 'cause there's a lot of detectives. They'll just pick you up. They picked me up, Rib, Rock I, and K 56 and they took us in, and they told us that they don't want to see us anymore 'cause the next time they're going to take us to the precinct and lock us up. Now I just go there for maybe a couple of minutes. It's a shame 'cause you can see a lot of real nice pieces there on the 2, the 4, and the 5. Now most people just ride the trains and get off somewhere to look.

5

Gangs and Groups

Gangs

New York City has long been plagued by the violence of street gangs. In 1972, for example, gangs in the Bronx were blamed by the police for 30 murders, 22 attempted homicides, 300 assaults, 10 rapes, and 124 armed robberies—actions that resulted in more than 1,500 arrests of gang members.[1] Such violent acts are generally directed against the members of rival gangs usually taking place during "rumbles," that, as described by the press, frequently amount to all-out warfare. As James Haskins has pointed out, however, "Gangs also commit their share of crimes 'just for kicks' . . . [engaging] in senseless acts of violence against innocent passers-by."[2] Young people in New York City, particularly those who live in lower-class neighborhoods, frequently are confronted by the choice of joining such gangs or becoming their victims.

Bama has described the gang situation as it existed when he lived in the Bronx in the early 1970s:

> The Savage Skulls, the Savage Nomads, the Seven Immortals, the Black Pearls, the Black Spades. Those were the main gangs, there were a lot more than that, but those were the main gangs in the Bronx you really had to look out for. And they had their big territories. The Bronx was broken up by those groups and the little gangs had their own little pockets like their neighborhoods. And up in the north Bronx where we were there was Intercrime, there were the Valley Boys. Every time I came home, I had to deal with that. So I became a Valley Boy. And to them I wasn't AMRL [the name he was writing at the time], I was a Valley Boy. And sometimes, we'd come up against the Edenwald Boys. Many of my good friends who were writers lived in Edenwald. So that was rough because every time I went up to pick up Moe TR I would have trouble with the Edenwald Boys and Intercrime, who were not the most reasonable people to deal with.

Bama's association with the Valley Boys did not last long, for as a serious graffiti writer, he could not afford to limit himself to the safety of a gang's limited turf and needed to be free to wander and write at large. That he was not affiliated with a rival gang was not enough to assure his safe passage through the maze of gang-controlled turfs and territories that covered the Bronx, so he devised this solution to his problem:

> What I did—this is one of the AMRL tricks, a trick of survival—is that I got to know people by going to certain places in the Bronx. You know, those hole-in-the-wall party places at the beginning of the disco era. So I'd go to these places on a Friday night in the Bronx and just party. They were grimy little places but it was just beautiful. I'd just be soaking up the atmosphere. Like there was this place on 169th Street called the Puzzle and a place on 161st Street called the Tunnel. These places catered to the high school people. Since it was in the Bronx you'd get to meet all the Bronx high school people when they were partying. A lot of them were in the gangs. . . . Like I'd see a cat who was a nut and I'd say, "Know him." I'd say, "Man what's your name," and he'd say, "I'm Killer," and I'd say, "I'm Bama, I write AMRL." And he'd say, "Yeah, I've seen your name." And I'd say, "Want me to hit your clubhouse or something, man?" And he'd say, "Yeah, that'd be nice." So that way I got to know everybody in most of the big gangs so I didn't have too many problems.

According to Bama, writers had little trouble with the big gangs like the Black Pearls because they were "too busy worrying about the other big gangs" to trouble themselves with the wanderings of mere graffiti writers. Also members of the big gangs, although acknowledged to be the "baddest guys around," never dared to leave their own turf except in large numbers, for to travel alone through a rival gang's territory was dangerous. When such gang members heard that writers often wandered alone and unarmed through every neighborhood in the Bronx, they began to respect them for what they saw as exceptional, if insane, courage. Bama has further explained this phenomenon:

> Take a Savage Skull. A Savage Skull fought like a Skull. You know: "I'm bad. I'll fuck you up. But I'm not walking out to University Avenue by myself." Here's AMRL who went and hit on University Avenue. "I'll give you heart, Bro. I seen your name in my neighborhood, but I also seen your name on University Avenue. That's crazy." To them

it's crazy because they can't do it, but I could. . . . They were all locked up in their neighborhoods and thinking that they were the baddest. Being the baddest, if they weren't going to do it, anyone who would was bad. So we got an instant reputation.

Taking advantage of their reputations with the big gangs, Bronx writers began to advertise their status as free agents by wearing denim graffiti jackets (patterned after the colors worn by gang members), on which they painted their names in colorful graffiti style. Some writers also began to attend the parties that the gangs frequently threw during school hours. Bama has described one such affair:

Like we used to have hooky parties at 152d Street and Third Avenue in an abandoned building. The Black Pearls took the basement and turned it into a nice little space to have parties. They'd have parties like from twelve o'clock to five o'clock and they'd charge you a quarter and graffiti artists were free. . . . Everybody in there had Black Pearls on their jackets. But if you came in with your graffiti jacket, you were cool. I mean you couldn't come in with a Black Spades jacket or a Savage Skulls jacket but you could go in if you were a writer. So at the party they'd say, . . . "the only people allowed in here are women, Black Pearls and graffiti writers." If you brought a friend, that was cool and if they had friends, that was O.K. too. But that was it. And it was a nice place. But one day the Black Spades came and that's when I realized we had respect because when they came they carried many guns. And they turned on all the lights and looked around and first they took and beat up a couple of guys because, though they weren't in a gang, they just needed a good ass-kicking at the time. Then they said, "All the graffiti artists, you, you, and you, split, because we don't want you guys to get involved. So you all just slip out." So we got out and when we got to the corner we heard bang, ting-a-ling, smash! But we just went upstairs, got on the train, made a tag, and went on about our business. But we didn't go back.

Areas that were not dominated by the large gangs were owned by small gangs whose territory often did not extend beyond a single block or corner, and it was with these status-hungry gangs that writers had the greatest trouble. Bama explains, "It was the little gangs that cause most of the problems because you didn't know who they were. You know, there'd be twenty-five people and they'd said, 'Let's become a gang. What do we do to become a gang? Well, we need a reputation. So let's fuck up six graffiti artists. The biggest ones that we can find.' So they'd do it and that way they got a reputation. So all over the school you'd hear, 'Did you hear what happened to Phase II and Sweet Duke? They got ripped up bad by these guys.' But that's how these gangs set about getting recognition." In encounters with the small gangs, the writers' only route to survival was to use their wits. Once Bama got into a confrontation when he and some other writers tagged on the wall of an apparently abandoned building that turned out to be the headquarters of a little gang:

Me and Iron Mike and all of us hit that clubhouse, and they were all inside and they got mad and they came down on us and they wheeled out these shotguns and they were gonna blow us away. No two buts about it. . . . They were mad. They were mad! They flung us up against these walls and put the guns at our chests. They wanted us to clean it first and then they were gonna blow us away. And that's what we had, was that edge on time, that they weren't going to fuck us up until we cleaned it. And that's how we got away. I talked our way out of it 'cause I just pushed them back and started talking and talking and talking and walking and talking and walking and talking until I got to the corner. I figured if I could get around the corner, I was all right. So I turned my back on them 'cause I figured they ain't gonna shoot me in the back if I just . . . walk away from these dudes after saying something heavy to them. Make them think for a second. . . . I came down on them. I told them how stupid they were. I told them to "just put the guns away 'cause you ain't gonna kill me for no hit on no clubhouse. I don't care how important it is to you." And I walked on that. And they looked at me and said "What the fuck?" which was long enough for me to get to the corner and disappear. 'Cause it just takes one step around the corner before you run. You know, a slow turn around the corner and as soon as you get out of sight, you vanish, you fly. And when I ran . . . that was their [the other writers'] cue and they just flipped. They booked in every different direction they could run in and they got away, we all got away.

Looking back on this incident and others, Bama has said: "It was dangerous but luckily I didn't run into much of it. I had my share but I didn't run into much of it. I'm still alive, so I didn't."

Writing Gangs

In Brooklyn the gang situation was even worse than in the Bronx. Bama's wanderings frequently took him to Brooklyn:

In Brooklyn, the groups that were out were very violent, the Jolly Stompers, the Tomahawks. . . . They were very violent groups. They weren't about just fucking up other gangs. They were attacking civilians, just the people. . . . that's something the other [Bronx] gangs didn't consider, you know, "You're not important; why should I mess with you? I got important people to worry about." And that's why we were able to be left alone except for the small little gangs. In Brooklyn there was a situation where the gangs were so bad that . . . the Tomahawks wouldn't go against the Jolly Stompers because the Tomahawks know that if they walked in there they were walking in there to shoot seventeen niggers. And they knew that the Jolly Stompers would not deal with getting sixteen or seventeen of the boys shot so there would be a good thirty or forty people shot up. So what did they do, they went and picked on other people to get their jock off. They were violent.

The writers in Brooklyn dealt with their problems with gangs in a direct manner: they formed gangs of their own. The first of these writing, as distinct from fighting, gangs was the Vanguards, formed early in 1971 in the Albany Projects of East Brooklyn. Soon after a second writing gang, the Last Survivors, was started in Fort Greene.

Although ostensibly formed only for the sake of writing and self-preservation, these writing gangs were similar to fighting gangs in that they sometimes purposefully engaged in rumbles with other gangs, limited membership to writers from their home turf and, in Wicked Gary's words, "Basically they were into fighting and dealing with their territory. They were into territory."

In late 1971 the Ex-Vandals, the first and only true writing gang, was formed. Although its members generally traveled in large groups and wore colors similar to those of fighting gangs, the Ex-Vandals existed solely for the purpose of writing graffiti and preserved itself through "safety in numbers" rather than violence.

The idea of forming the Ex-Vandals originated with seven experienced Brooklyn writers: Dino Nod, Wicked Gary, Flin, King of Kools, Wicked Wesley, Big Time Glass-Top, and Conrad Is Bad. Wicked Gary, former vice-president of the gang, recalled their first meeting:

Seven of us all from Erasmus [High School, Brooklyn] decided we would get together because we were writers anyway. We were thinking about the fact that here we were writing seven different names all over the place and they were around and people were seeing them and everything, but what would happen if we got together and wrote one name and put it everywhere and the effect it would have? So that's what we set out to do. So one Friday afternoon, Dino Nod, who was the leader and the originator of the idea, said, "Let's go by my house after school and sit down and get a name together and whatever else we want to do." So we had a meeting between the seven of us. . . . At the meeting the first thing we decided was that we wanted a name, something that would be dynamic, something that would have the effect that we wanted so we said, "Let's choose something that fits us," and we were talking about the name *Vanguard*, and *Vandals* came up. Somebody was being sarcastic and said, "You know, like we're Vandals, destroying property, so they say." And we said, "Yeah, we hear you." Then we started thinking that we were all writers and we've all been out there, so we were all experienced, so after a while of floating around, we shortened *Experienced* to *Ex* and we liked *Vandals* so here we were, Experienced Vandals, the Ex-Vandals. Then we decided to think up some letters to go with it, like a say-

ing. And we came up with WBYA—"We Bust Your Ass."
And that was the formation of the first *graffiti* group. All
the other writers who were dealing with groups were dealing with gang-type groups who were fighters along with
writers. . . . The only purpose of the Vandals was for writing. And that was established right away. And "we bust
your ass" was about the fact that nobody who was a writer
could top us 'cause we were some of the best.

The seven decided that the best way to promote their
group and attract new members was to arouse fellow writers'
curiosity by getting the gang's name up as much as possible
while keeping their own identities secret. Over the weekend
following their first meeting, they executed their first "graffiti
blitz," writing their gang name everywhere they could both in
the area of their school and in their individual neighborhoods.
The response that these actions evoked from their fellow students was powerful: "They came back over the weekend and
everywhere they went they saw 'Ex-Vandals,' 'Ex-Vandals,'
'Ex-Vandals.' 'What are the Ex-Vandals? Who are they?
Where did this come from?' Come Monday . . . we had a cult
thing happening because nobody knew who we were, everybody saying, 'What's happening?' 'Who's the Ex-Vandals?' "
And after a week of writing and waiting, the seven revealed
themselves:

> We finally broke it to everybody by getting our dungaree
> jackets. We decided, "O.K., we got all the interest now.
> Let's break out one at a time and show them who we are
> and see what develops." Everybody painted the dungaree
> jackets with *Ex-Vandals* and their name, and one by one
> we wore them to school. And then they found out who we
> were and we were put up on a pedestal. . . . So we were
> this elite group, and we kept it like that, kept our member-
> ship doors closed until we picked who we wanted to join
> us. And then we started expanding, getting others in-
> volved.

After a month twenty new members had joined, and the
leaders of the Ex-Vandals (the seven original members, with
Dino Nod as president) decided to test their gang's capabilities
and establish a reputation by engaging in a writing competi-

tion with Brooklyn's best-known fighting-and-writing gangs. Wicked Gary recalled the contest:

> We set up a competition with the Vanguards on who could get around the most writing their names. . . . Now the Vanguards had a lot of writers, and we decided the thing would be to define very quickly who were the kings of the territory. . . . We set a judging date for the competition. We gave ourselves a couple of months to battle the Vanguards for the claim of who was the best. So that gave us a lot of time to work on everything that we were doing and be organized. . . . We would have meetings regularly at Nod's house. We decided to make Fridays our regular meeting day and we would just leave school together and go to Nod's house after school and decide what we were going to hit and we would divide it up. We figured out a plan to get the whole Brooklyn area, and we didn't just limit it to Brooklyn. We used to take subway maps and street maps and plot out what areas we wanted to hit, and we would be able to say by the next week, "We did this area and this area; we have to go here now." . . . We crushed them. It was unanimous; they didn't have the places that we had. They didn't have the power that we had. We were not only into hitting a lot. We used to hit what you would call fantabulous spots, places that other people wouldn't think of. When you looked at it, it would have an effect that would awe you and make your mouth drop open. Dino Nod used to be very good for that 'cause no matter where he'd go, he'd find a spot to put in *Ex-Vandals*, places up high, places far away which you wouldn't expect nobody to get. . . . One of the things that we worked on was if you were in a place and you saw the name of the Vanguards, we wanted you to see the name of the Vandals right there. . . . So we would cover all their hits, matching everything that they did, plus more. . . . So no matter what name was up, if it was a group or if there was maybe nothing there but toy stuff, we'd put something there that had some force behind it which was Ex-Vandals. They had to admit it themselves 'cause they'd go out to Queens, they would go to Manhattan, they would go to the Bronx, and

they'd be riding the trains. They could go all over and they could see the Vandals. . . . The Vanguards were out there but not as much so they had no claim.

The Ex-Vandals's victory over the Vanguards enhanced their growing reputation among writers throughout the city. Self-appointed independent members wrote the gang's name in the Bronx, Manhattan, and Queens. The Ex-Vandals's core membership in Brooklyn also grew, and the leaders of the gang devised a plan whereby they could take full advantage of their increased strength.

There was so much interest in it that a lot of people really wanted to be in the group just to say they were part of the Vandals. And what we did with those people was we made them work. A lot of times the seven of us would take groups out into different areas and supervise the hitting, making sure that we got done what we had in our gang plan and doing all the added stuff that would give us the power to do what we had to do. . . . Even though I didn't really know the subways that well because I wasn't riding them, I had the ideas of how to organize it so that we could get to the whole city about all at once. I devised methods where we could go in teams and get whole subway lines in a night. . . . We had a master gang plan, and we had that all mapped out, the strategy and everything. It was like an army. It was volunteer. We'd say, "We're opening our doors, would you like to join?" Once you got their interest and they'd come in, you'd train them, develop them, and get them to do the job along with us. I felt that the most efficient way to deal with the subways was to go in teams, almost like tag teams in wrestling. . . . If you had a team of four, you could get two guys to cover you and block people's vision while you hit. We could look out for each other too because the team that was getting off the train could signal whether there was a cop or something. So we could give a whistle or some kind of message that would say, "Stay," or "Get on the train and we'll meet at the next stop." Communication was happening. With the alternating stations we didn't have to get off at every stop so we could move right along. And since there were four of us, we could divide the train—some of us take the front, some the ends, some the middle. Then we'd get on another train, a big group, go on another two stops, get off, check out the security for the other team. It was constant. . . . We'd try to be very discreet. Also we were very fast. If you'd blink and then look up, you'd see a hit and you wouldn't know how it got there.

Among its many new members, the Ex-Vandals counted a number of females. Wicked Gary mentioned some of them:

We had a bunch of girls in our group . . . about twenty or twenty-five. They used to use boys' names when they wrote. Daring Danny was a girl named Denise. Bad Bobby was a girl named Robin. Long Lightnin' Larry was a girl named Lynn. Mighty Mike was a girl named Michelle. They were like sisters, cousins, friends who lived in the neighborhood and they were writers too, so we got them involved and they became Ex-Vandals. . . . I myself used to go spraying with a girl named Dimples, she was my partner. . . . We'd carry a couple of cans of paint and markers. And we'd ride the trains as a couple. If cops came in the back or anything, we'd be in the corner like man and woman with paint behind us in the corner, like, "Ain't nothing happening with us 'cept what you see." And the cop might come in and he'd look at us and smell all this fresh marker and paint and he would wonder what was happening but he couldn't say anything to us 'cause he didn't see us do anything and he couldn't just accuse us. Sometimes also we'd mislead him, like, "There was some kids on a couple of stops ago and they got off . . . but you might be able to catch them." So then they'd get off at the next stop and they would be long gone and we would just do what we wanted to do.

By spring 1972 the ranks of the Ex-Vandals had grown substantially and the leaders decided the time had come for the gang to show its unity and numbers to the rest of the city. The forum chosen for this demonstration was opening day at Coney Island. Wearing their colors, dungaree jackets and jeans painted with various designs and the gang's and individual members' names, seventy Ex-Vandals gathered at a

Burger Master restaurant near Brooklyn's Prospect Park, their headquarters, on Easter morning. The events that followed were recounted by Wicked Gary:

> The day on Easter, on the boardwalk, was one of the most frightening days I had as a Vandal. We met at our usual headquarters and got on the train. We got everybody organized and we went to Coney Island with all our colors. This was the first time we'd gone out as a big group to show a little power, a little support. We had sent out a team the week before to kill Coney Island, so when we got down there with all the other groups there would be "Vandals" all over the place, on the top of buildings and on all the games and rides and all this other stuff. That was our time to show the city who we were. We had already shown Brooklyn. . . . On the train . . . we met one of the divisions of the Black Spades. I don't remember what division of the Black Spades [the largest of the Bronx street gangs] it was, but there was about twenty of them on the train. And since we were a writing group, we said, "Hey, Black Spades." And we met them and learned their names and we wrote their names out. So we got a little friendship thing happening with them which was very good for us because we understood that they were going out to meet all the rest of their divisions at Coney Island.
>
> Coney Island on Easter Sunday is a place to go for the youths. You've got all these games around and amusement and stuff is happening; it's something that people do in the city. The gangs say, "We could show some power, so let's go down there in a unified group." That's what we were doing and that's what they were doing, and that's what all the other gangs were doing.
>
> So when we got down there, we stayed together as a group. We went around and rode on the rides together and we finally got to the boardwalk. And it was like, "This is all right, let's stretch out and take up the whole width of the boardwalk. Let's walk with our colors now. Strut, take your time and strut." Everybody was like turning their heads, mouths dropping. People were like getting out of our way, they didn't know what was happening. We felt good because we had all this so-called instant power and it

wasn't destructive or nothing like that, but there was a lot of ego playing. We were playing with our own egos and it was fun.

And everybody was looking at us but then after a while they were looking through us and past us, like behind us. And I was wondering like, "What the hell was all this about?" 'cause we were getting close to the end of the boardwalk, and even though we were a major sight, all of a sudden it didn't seem like we were important no more. So when we got to the boardwalk and we turned around, we saw all the divisions of the Black Spades were behind us. Everybody said, "Oh, shit!" because it was a sea of people. They had like rows of people covering the same width we were covering—the whole boardwalk which is a very wide boardwalk.

We stopped in our tracks. We didn't take not another step. It was like, "What's gonna happen?" People were watching just to see what was going to happen. But up front was the division we saw on the train and you have never seen us so happy. "Hey, what's happening? How you doing?" So that cooled that whole thing out because they had asked us on the train, "What are you all about? Are you all like a fighting group or what?" But we had explained we were just a writing group, and our thing is getting our name around and we're not into fighting and all this, and we took the time to explain it and it paid off. That's the one thing we kept stressing to everybody—that we were not a fighting group and no matter what you were doing, we weren't about fighting, even if you were coming at us, threatening us, we weren't about fighting. It really got played off 'cause they had like so many hot rocks you wouldn't believe. Even the members we had met on the train had sawed-off shotguns, chains, knives, anything you could think of they had with them. I mean they were a gang. A serious gang. The leader of the gang we had met on the train had a sawed-off shotgun and some other stuff, walking around with it in a shopping bag. It wasn't nothing to him 'cause he had some light stuff compared to what some of his boys and girls had.

And they had a division of girls; they had some girls with them too. And they looked harder than some of the dudes. I swear to God. And one of the things that played it off so well was that our girls were basically good looking 'cause they were into themselves. And since they weren't about fighting, they didn't have to be like hard rocks and they could still be girls and have something about them, like shape and jiggle and all that stuff happening. And the Spades were like, "Hey man, I'm gonna join the Vandals; you see their women?" And they're looking over their shoulders at some of the girls they had with them, and we hit it off very well because of that.

A little bit later a fight broke out between the Black Spades and a white gang from one of the projects. There was a big rumble in the projects. And the cops were going around rounding everybody up who was wearing dungaree jackets and colors. But that even worked out because when all the gangs were doing their running, we happened to run into them and they told us that the cops were looking for people and turn our colors inside out and cool out, which helped us out 'cause we didn't get into any trouble. But we would have been involved if they hadn't warned us. . . . At that time the Black Spades had over forty divisions. There were representatives of every division out there that day but we didn't have any trouble with them.

The Ex-Vandals were not always as fortunate in their dealings with Brooklyn street gangs. In one case, a conflict with one of the smaller fighting gangs resulted in a face-to-face full-strength confrontation. Wicked Gary recalled the incident:

It was a toy gang, I forget the name of it. They decided that they didn't like us and they were going to get us, so they put the word out in advance and what they were planning on doing was coming to our headquarters and setting us straight that they didn't like us. . . . We had our hangout at the Burger Master. . . . It was a good location for us because we could hit buses and trains and still deal with hanging out . . . and we had the park too. But they used to have to go by there when they took the bus when they were going home, so we decided one day that we weren't going to take no shit from them. We'd get everybody together and we'd wait for them one day, just wait for them and find out what they got to say. The Black Dragons was their name, yeah, the Black Dragons.

So there was about ninety of us waiting in the parking lot at Wetson's. We decided not to go into Burger Master but to hang out in Wetson's parking lot because there weren't so many people there waiting for buses. . . . I saw a train pull up and about twenty-five [Black Dragons] got out and we saw them file into our headquarters. So we decided to let them all get in there and then go in there and close the entrance off and find out what was happening. They went in there and ordered their food and started eating when ninety of us piled in, walked around them, and stood around them and everything. There were so many of us that people couldn't get into the store. The lady behind the counter knew us all and she asked us, "Please, whatever you do, don't start nothing in here." But we said, "No, we aren't gonna start nothing, this is our headquarters." They lost their appetite for their food. They lost their appetite for everything. . . . We had no problems.

Although the Ex-Vandals came out on top in their conflict with the Black Dragons, their strength-in-numbers theory was not as successful in their dealings with larger gangs. Eventually their difficulties with a number of big fighting gangs forced them to disband. Wicked Gary outlined the demise of the Ex-Vandals:

Some of the . . . gangs that were more serious decided that they were going to get on our case. Not the Vanguards because they always stayed our friends, but the Jolly Stompers and the Tomahawks decided that they didn't like what was happening. And they put out the word that it's open season on the Vandals and there used to be a lot of trouble because a lot of people who wanted to be in the group were afraid to use the name and there were a lot of conflicts that came out of it. A couple of people got hurt. I know that one night Nod was at the skating rink at the Rollerdome. And about fifty Jolly Stompers were at the rink and they recognized Nod and they chased him home which was roughly about three blocks but they were after him. But Nod was crazy enough to come back downstairs with a big tomahawk and confront them. "Come on with you."

. . . The people put us on so much of a pedestal that it was really something to be an Ex-Vandal; it was like being part of the royal court, and that doesn't do anybody's ego who isn't part of the group any good. So that's where the fighting energies came through in trying to knock us down and just do anything they could to try and destroy what we had. If they couldn't be part of it they'd . . . eliminate us. Eventually the group got split up because of the ideas that happened. After a while Nod just sort of like gave up with dealing with the group anymore, but I tried to keep it happening until finally I said, "The hell with it," myself. I felt I couldn't do but so much more with it because we had already expanded to Manhattan and the Bronx and we were getting numbers and it was over, it was like in the papers and stuff. And this was around 1972.

By the time the Ex-Vandals folded, its saturation techniques and wide-ranging coverage had made its name famous. The example of the Ex-Vandals was an important influence on the later formation of graffiti groups, and today the writers of a much later generation still talk about the Ex-Vandals. Many think of it, as does Apollo 5, as "the greatest group that ever was. I wish I'd been in it."

The success of the Ex-Vandals has also had an influence on the attitudes of some of the fighting gangs toward writing. Gangs have used graffiti to mark their turf since time immemorial, but their graffiti writing generally was limited to a few well-placed hits at the fringes of their territories. When the Ex-Vandals got fame, however, the gangs, who always were interested in finding ways to enhance their reputations, began to do more extensive writing of their own. Fred, who began his writing career as a gang member, has told of the influence that Ex-Vandals-style writing had on his gang:

Now the gang I was in, the Hellcats, their main function was to beat people up. We ran Bed-Stuy; the Tomahawks had Brownsville. Our turf was so vast that we had divisions. Like I was in the 113 Hellcats. Then there was the

104 division and that had three divisions in it. One time we all came together for a massive rumble and we were 2,000 people. I couldn't believe it. They all weren't wearing colors. But you could tell they were Hellcats because we all had this burn on our arms, like Kool, who was the prez, he'd take a cigarette and put it out on your arm, and you'd rub the skin and there was white meat there and it'd leave this mark. When they made me the head of the writing section, I had to get one on my chest.

Once you got all drunked up it didn't hurt much. And once you got it, you was down. But when I look back at it now, it was like a social thing and a status thing. Like if you was an Ex-Vandal, you was known. Just for writing on walls you was known. A famous writer could go into any area of Brooklyn and get respect.

You have to understand that if you see something and you know it visually, you're as aware of it as if you hear something about a gang. Like if the Tomahawks did a brutal killing, then they were known as a brutal gang and you knew their name for that reason. But the Ex-Vandals' name was all over the walls and so you knew about them as well. So they had plenty of pull too. But a lot of the fighting gangs looked at them as faggots. "What you writing on walls for?" But when they saw that it was good to get your gang known, they started writing too. That's how I started doing it. I was part of the Hellcats when I started writing and I said, "Why not write the name of the gang too?" And they really liked it. Then other people wrote too. Like in a gang everybody took a name. Like Kool, Speedy, Ice, Lucky, Phantom, you know, names like that. So then they all started writing their names, and I formed a writing division and we started pairing off and doing a lot of writing.

On the surface, writers have a good deal in common with gang members. Both seek recognition from their peers, use aliases, take part generally in illegal activities, see themselves as noble outlaws, are young, are most often poor. Graffiti writers also fit James Haskins's observations about the primary motivations behind gang activity: "Participation in gang activities is one way of feeling like 'somebody.' Identity, a sense of belonging, a sense of importance—for many in the lower economic classes . . . gang activity has seemed the only way to fulfill these very important needs."[3] The main difference between gang members and writers is that the former derive their sense of self from violence while the latter draw theirs from writing on walls and trains. Fred, who has experienced both worlds, commented, "A violent revolution should be the result of what people are forced to go through. But graffiti is what came out of it. Instead of taking arms we just took paint. There's some violence in the art; you can see it in the reds and oranges. But it has to be expressed. Looking over the past ten years, I can't see how it couldn't have been done. If there hadn't been graffiti, there would have been a lot more violence."

Groups

At approximately the time that the Ex-Vandals was being disbanded in Brooklyn, the first writing groups began to appear around the city. Unlike the writing gangs, these groups are rather informal in structure, have no hierarchy of officers, do not require members to wear identifying colors, and were not formed for the sake of defense against fighting gangs but only for companionship and occasional joint writing ventures. Group members also consider the writing of their own names to be far more important than getting their group's name up.

As the painting of pieces has gained in popularity and style wars have begun taking place, many writers find it necessary to spend long hours in the train yards perfecting their techniques. Going to the yards in groups provides these writers with companionship, help in watching for raids by the "DTs" (yard detectives), and extra hands to aid in the rapid completion of particularly large pieces.

Stan 153 was a member of the Three Yard Boys, one of Manhattan's first groups:

> The Three Yard Boys was a group of writers who lived around the 3 Yards [storage yards for IRT number 3 line trains]. This was Jace 2, Rome 150, Hace 150, Lace 150, Mike 150, myself, and Fun 161. These were the original Three Yard Boys, though there were more later. We shortly abbreviated the name to 3YB. The reason we named ourselves the Three Yard Boys is because on the other side of

Caine, calling himself "the bad artist!"
tags up the names of the three groups
to which he belongs. Henry Chalfant

the 3 yard is a fence and we opened up so many holes in it that the cops didn't know which one to watch and we could always get in. Like we'd cut a hole and then leave the fence part there and just pull it back like a door when we wanted to get in. We also had a ledge that overlooked the whole yard so we could see what was going on, so when we were in there a lookout could say, "There's a cop on the third lane!" and then we could run out. In a sense we did own the yard. About half the yard was ours. But the rest, who cares?

With the advent of whole-car painting, many groups have divided the labor necessary for creating them. Portions of the work are doled out according to the skill and status of the writers. Graffiti squad officer Conrad Lesnewski explains:

Kids will work on these in a group. Each kid has his own job and knows what to do. They'll have a work order. . . . They will bring to a job exactly as much paint as they need . . . and they'll farm it out, they'll say, "You bring two cans of hot pink, you, three cans of some sort of green," that's each one doing his job. . . . The new ones they'll just give the mopping up, filling in the colors, or something. Sometimes when you catch a kid or make a raid, one kid will say, "I wasn't painting, I was just filling in." He doesn't consider himself painting because the other guy did the artwork.

When groups go to the yard with the intention of doing individual pieces, they are far less organized. Because limited open space is available on the trains, disagreements often arise over who will get the "good spots," the area under the windows being most highly prized. Bama has explained how decisions on space allotment are sometimes made: "Usually the bigger writer will say, 'That's my spot, you don't fuck with it.' And they write and the little writers, the toys at the time, will watch, and whatever space you leave them they'll hit. . . . When . . . the big writers are out it's like *Star Wars.* 'I want this spot.' 'No, it's mine!' They would . . . try to paint as fast as they could so they could get as much space as they need."

Groups form in a number of ways. Most consist of writers of about the same level of skill who meet in school or in their neighborhoods and decide to "hook up a group" together. Toy groups, for example, consist of inexperienced writers who decide to work jointly toward developing their writing techniques and building their reputations, often doing much of their early work on paper or on walls in their neighborhoods. Most toys, however, get their start by joining open-membership groups that usually consist of one or two skilled master artists who manage a large group of student writers. The leaders of such groups benefit by acquiring willing workers who assist them in their writing and, often, steal paint for them. The toys profit by having an opportunity to learn from an experienced writer and also, possibly, by having some of their teacher's status rub off on them. Police officer Lesnewski explained the manner in which such groups operate:

> They initiate them by having them steal the paint and they'll teach them how not to be apprehended. The younger boy is called a toy when he's just starting out into graffiti. If the older person, the leader, cares for him, he'll teach him how to walk on the tracks, how to "run the board," they call it, and how to run between the cars, how to shimmy down an el pole when the cops start to chase him, how to go in between the railroad tracks. An actual training course, like. If he's good enough, if he has style, then he'll be accepted with the organization. If he has real style, very, very good, then he can belong to any organization you want, any place in the city. Not only your local area, but from here to Brooklyn, from Brooklyn to Manhattan, or the Bronx and so on.

The memberships of such groups change constantly as new writers join and others, having become skilled writers in their own right, form their own groups or accept invitations to join higher-level groups.

The most admired graffiti groups are the master groups that consist only of highly skilled and experienced writers. The Fabulous Five is the most famous of these groups, and its membership, with the exception of a visit by an occasional "guest star," has remained unchanged for more than four years. When asked to name the members of the Fabulous

Five, practically every writer can rattle off their names like the lyrics of a familiar song: Lee, Mono, Doc, Slave, and Slug. All five of these writers are over eighteen years of age and plan to retire soon. When they do, as Lee has put it, "We're gonna take the name with us—nobody else should ever use it. There is only one Fabulous Five."

Other master groups have managed to achieve a sort of immortality by selectively bringing in promising new writers to replace those who retire. In this way the Three Yard Boys has managed to keep its name and reputation alive since 1972. Stan 153, an original 3YB, does not know any of the current members of the group but has said, "I've seen their stuff on the trains and it's all right. Not as good as we were, but they're keeping the name alive and there's pride in that."

One advantage of being part of a master group is that its members enjoy the freedom to travel to yards throughout the city to do their painting. Many groups stake claims on particular yards or lay-ups and attempt to build their reputations by "bombing" one selected train line. Such groups jealously hold on to what they consider to be their exclusive rights to painting in these areas and will run off groups that attempt to trespass in them. Police officers Hickey and Lesnewski explain:

Hickey:
> A lot of the kids will, by and large, stay in one area on one line . . .

Lesnewski:
> Except the big groups . . . Lee and Mono, Doc, Slave and Slug, the Fabulous Five. They go any place they want in the city. Brooklyn, the New Lots yard, all the way up to the 241st Street yards, and any other groups in there, when they see them, they know who they are and they'll move out of the way for them or they'll join them so they can say, "I was painting with Lee, I was with Lee last night. I helped him do that."

Hickey:
> If a new group goes into an area, like if a group from the Bronx goes into Brooklyn . . . the group from the Brooklyn area would accost them, might beat them up, but would definitely steal their paint.

Conflicts arise between groups. Toy groups frequently are set upon and have their paint stolen by groups of older writers. Other groups sometimes fight in a yard over the rights to a clean train. In such situations, group members are expected to stand together. For example, if one member of a group is backgrounded, fellow group members are expected to assist in paying back the offender by crossing out his pieces and sometimes those of members of any groups with which he is associated. They in turn all seek revenge and such a matter can escalate into a cross-out war in which members of both groups background each other at a furious rate until, as Dea-2 has put it, "They call a truce . . . for the sake of the art."

Conflicts sometimes arise even between well-known groups. Stan 153 has described one such conflict between the Three Yard Boys and another large Manhattan group, the Soul Artists: "One night the 3YB and the Soul Artists met at a playground near the Three Yard. Our relations were a little bit shaky. They wanted to fight us. But since I was there I said, 'Listen fellas, no fighting. Let's just sit down, play a game of basketball.' Everybody played some basketball and then we decided to go piece together. We all had paint, and that night we converged together and became as one. It was a beautiful feeling and there were some amazing pieces done."

For writers who want to start a group, coming up with a good name for it is of primary importance. As Tracy 168 has said, "If you want a group to grow, the name's gotta be good . . . strong, the kind of name you want to have up there with yours." A group with an appealing name frequently will draw many members on that basis alone. As the group grows larger and more people write the name, the group stands a chance of becoming famous, bringing status to all of its members.

A writer who comes up with a good group name frequently will try it out on others, hoping that they will like it and write it. In the years following the demise of the Ex-Vandals, Wicked Gary thought of a number of new group names but none of them attracted much attention. One time, he said, "I came up with DEAD, which is supposed to be 'Dedicated and Experienced and Altogether' and anything you can think of with a *D* like *devastating* or *destructive*, *daring*, anything you wanted you had the option of to put on the end. But that didn't come

"Title box" of a whole car painted by the members of the United Artists group. Henry Chalfant

off that tough. I told Lazar, and he wrote it a couple of times and I wrote it a couple of times. But I don't know if anybody else got involved with it."

When writers decide to affiliate with a group, they usually sign its name, or more often its initials, after or below their own names. New groups appear and others vanish, seemingly daily, but at present the group names and initials that appear most frequently on the subways are the following:

Three Yard Boys (3YB)
Six Yard Boys (6YB)
The Burners (TB)
The Spanish Five (TSF)
The Art Partners
The Nasty Artists (TNA)
Mass Transit Boys (MT Boys)
The Crew (TC)
Stone Killers (SK)
Salsa Boys (SB)
The Crazy Artists (TCA)
The Independents (IND's)
The Bronx Boys (TBB)
The Untouchables
Challenge to Be Free
Destroy All Trains (DAT)
The Smokin' Partners
The Killers

The Rebels (TR)
The Ebony Dukes
Wild Styles
Raw Writers (RW)
The Equal Brothers (EB)
Wanted
Mad Transit Artists (MTA)
The Fabulous Five
Mission Graffiti (MG)
The Master Crew (TMC)
The Kool Artists (TKA)
The Death Squad (TDS)
The Fabulous Crew (TFC)
The Incredible Crew (TIC)
The Rainbow Brothers (TRB)
Master Blasters (MB)
The Mob (TM)
The Bad Artists (TBA)

There are scores, possibly hundreds, of other names that appear less frequently. There is, in fact, such a plethora of groups about that a writer may join a number of them, tagging one or another or all of their names, depending on his mood. Son One is in a couple of groups: "You don't stick to just one group because it gets dull." In fact many writers "write a group," signing its name along with their own simply because they like the name, not because they have joined it.

Some writers find such an attitude toward group membership deplorable. Lee of the Fabulous Five and Caz, formerly of the Nasty Brothers, recently discussed the current state of groups:

Caz:

There's too many. It's like guys say, "Hey, they got a group. We write so let's form a group too." It used to be that when people were in a group they stayed with it and went out as a group. Today people write all sorts of groups.

Lee:

Groups don't even care for each other. Like "If you go over my boy's name, I'll go over you."

Caz:

In my group, TNB, we ended up with only two people, and the other guy wouldn't even stick up for me. So I write for myself now. I won't put up a group name anymore.

6

Organizations

Yolanda Rodriguez

In a few instances writers have assembled or been gathered into groups or organizations formed for the purpose of redirecting writers from train painting toward more socially acceptable forms of artistic expression. Usually started by adults, such organizations have sought to help writers develop their artistic abilities and invest their creativity in potentially profitable endeavors. The organizations have sought to legitimize graffiti style and win their members recognition as serious artists by encouraging writers to produce graffiti-style works on canvas and various other media with a view toward their sale to art collectors and the general public.

Such organizations generally have been enthusiastically received by the writers, and though they have not yet enjoyed great financial success, they have played an important role in directing numerous writers toward college study and careers in art. Organizations have as well served as an important means of socializing, for writers from different parts of the city to meet and get to know each other.

The two most successful and widely known of these organizations are the now-defunct United Graffiti Artists (UGA), the first of them and the only one that limited membership to master artists, and the Nation of Graffiti Artists (NOGA), which had a broad membership.

United Graffiti Artists

In fall 1972 Hugo Martinez, a junior and a sociology major at City College in Manhattan, decided to form an organization of graffiti artists. Martinez had spent the previous summer working as a teacher for the Queens College Summer Program, a federally funded precollege program for disadvantaged city youths. Martinez had been assigned by the program to work with young Hispanics, and it was there that he "realized the vast potential of Puerto Rican adolescents and what they might achieve by rechanneling their energies and interests. Also, I concluded that if any constructive work was to be done with these adolescents it must be with those who showed definite signs of rebellion, of a concentration on their own needs rather than the needs of traditional education."[1] He was convinced that the majority of writers were Puerto Rican teenagers, and he decided to test his theories by attempting to gather the most talented of them into an organization in which they could mutually work toward realizing their potential as artists. Martinez also apparently intended to use information gathered through work with the group as the basis for a sociological study.

Martinez's work with the Queens College program had put him in touch with members of the Young Galaxies, a Manhattan street gang. Henry 161, the gang's "public relations expert," and Freddie 173, a gang member and occasional graffiti writer, showed him their neighborhood's graffiti landmarks' "hidden caves, secret hitting places, school yards, 'signing-in' walls and tremendous feats: 'Saint 173' high on the wall of a hospital (painted while dangling over the roof). Freddie pointed out the names of the masters with reverent admiration: Hitler II, Baby Face 86, Cay 161, Turok . . . real heroes."[2] The tour ended at the popular writers' corner at 188th Street, where Martinez was introduced to Stitch I and Snake I, president and vice-president, respectively, of the corner, and Cat 87, all master writers, who received him "with silent suspicion and an air of being used to admiration, of expecting it."[3]

Martinez visited the corner regularly, befriending the writers there and learning "the secrets of graffiti: the moral codes, esthetic criteria, technology, nomenclature, history, legend and ritual."[4] Although the more prominent writers regarded him with suspicion, Martinez convinced a few of them to participate in a graffiti-writing demonstration at City College. He then acquired, with the help of one of his professors, the use of a large classroom and sufficient wrapping paper and spray paint to cover its ten by forty foot wall. On October 20, 1972, twelve writers entered the classrooms and hit their names legally for the first time:

> Once they realized the possibilities, all vestiges of street cool went out the window. They were ecstatic. The presence of so many masters together, all the spray paint and so much room to hit created a state of controlled frenzy.
>
> By the end of the work it was obvious that, given the amount of space, the legitimate surface and the mutual respect of professionals, the product was esthetically pleasing while maintaining its energy and impact. United Graffiti Artists was born.[5]

Of the twelve writers who took part in the demonstration, Martinez selected Snake I, Stitch I, Cat 87, and Co-Co as UGA's first members. The recruitment of other members was left to them and they selected Lee 163, Flint 707, Mico, Phase II, Wicked Gary, SJK 171, T-Rex 131, and Bama, all master writers. Shortly thereafter Co-Co was elected president of the organization and Bama vice-president.

Although during the three years of its existence, hundreds of applications for membership in UGA were received from writers throughout the city, the organization never had more than about twenty members at any given time and the original twelve remained, constituting its core membership and leadership.

UGA received its first publicity when the *New York Times* covered an exhibition that the organization held at City College's Eisner Hall in December 1972. Shortly thereafter UGA received and accepted an offer of $600 from Joffrey Ballet choreographer Twyla Tharp to take part in a production entitled "Deuce Coupe." The writers' role in the ballet was described by the Wall Street Journal: "While the dancers performed to pop music, Co-Co and his friends (the UGA artists) sprayed their names and other embellishments to create a flamboyant and fascinating backdrop. As the graffiti writers took their bows, waving their cans of spray paint, the trendy, avant-garde Joffrey audience responded with loud applause and numerous enthusiastic bravos. 'They're so real!' one young spectator exclaimed to his date."[6] Both the ballet and UGA's painting were praised widely in the press. Few other jobs materialized, however, and the group sorely needed funds for materials and working space. UGA had been meeting in the SoHo loft of an off-Broadway theater director, Jack Pelsinger, who had taken an interest in the group after their City College exhibition, but they and he had been, in Bama's words, "kicked out of the loft because people were writing on the outside of his apartment and they blamed us for it." The group was thus forced to move its operations to Martinez's one-bedroom apartment on West 89th Street in Manhattan. The Daily News described one of their typical meetings: "Martinez's wife Robin and their six-month-old son, whose nickname is Eric 89, look on while kids from 14 to 21 sit everywhere painting and sketching their names and numbers."[7]

Martinez's apartment was crowded, so he applied to a number of city agencies for a donation of studio space. Meanwhile he arranged for the UGA members to attend the Queens College summer program, from which they received a small stipend for living expenses. Bama said about the experience:

It was nice. They tried to teach us about art, our heritage, in the corniest way they could. But that was where we hung out . . . and we got closer . . . . Queens College wouldn't accept us. Everything that happened was on us again. A lot of it was our fault because we were goofing off. . . . Me and Ray B had this language, this pig Latin, where we put "izz" on the end of everything after the first letter. So for "mother," we'd say "mizzother." We'd get our little check and the crew chief would say, "What are you going to do with your money, Raymond?" "I'm going to buy some smizzoke and some cizzoke and get fizzuk tizzup." "Huh? Well, that's very good." "I know." Yeah, and they were going crazy, 'cause everything we said was in that language and they didn't like it. They isolated us, they put us way in the back of the campus and they made Hugo our teacher because no one else could deal with us . . . and from that we had freedom to just roam around the campus and cool out and have fun. Fun, fun, fun.

At the end of the summer, UGA finally got its studio, a loft in upper Manhattan with its rent to the city set at one dollar per year. The studio was in less than perfect condition, and the work in renovating it brought a new sense of seriousness and purpose to the group. As Bama described it:

It was a toy factory that had closed down in 1957. All this garbage was stacked in there for fifteen years and we had to clean this place up. . . . When we walked in there we had Pistol I in the group and he said "Fuck this!" and split. And a few other people who talked about getting into the group left the group and that's when UGA became strong because when those guys left, we were a unit now of twelve people. Those twelve people cleaned up that studio. . . . We had to become in that little time carpenters, sanitation men, floor experts, wall experts, electricians, plumbers; we did all the work.

Work on the studio did pull the group together, but conflicts also began to arise, Wicked Gary explained:

> It got to be a thing where Hugo got it into a Latino or Hispanic type of organization. Because what was set up was a big interracial thing between the Hispanics and the blacks and the whites and everything else. It got to be very awkward. . . . The fact was that Hugo is of a background and he was biased racially in terms of that background. We had to deal with those racial tensions too. We were all searching for our identity and that was part of it. If we were making suggestions for another member, like a black member, it was always a big controversy.

Conflicts also arose over admitting women to the organization. Bama has described Martinez's and some of the other members' attitudes toward Stoney, a well-known female writer from Brooklyn who was a UGA member for a few months:

> With Stoney it was just about her being a woman because she was a good woman and she was strong and she was about the work. And I think that's what got her out of it. If she had acted more feminine and you know, played this role of the chick, she would have still hung out. But she was about doing something, she was about working, she was about painting, and she was about being serious. Hugo kind of saw her as a threat to the other guys' egos because she kind of painted very very well. Like he didn't have to teach her how to stretch canvas. He told her, you're gonna have to stretch your own but he didn't show her how to do it. So she went out and did it. That sort of attitude that made some of the fellas who weren't as good but were important members of the group feel bad. So they felt that it would be good to get rid of her, and they got rid of her.

As work on the studio proceeded, Martinez arranged for UGA to present an exhibition of graffiti-style canvases at the Razor Gallery in SoHo. Opening on September 15, 1973, the show included more than twenty canvases by individual UGA members and an enormous group painting to which all of the members had contributed. The paintings were priced from

$200 to $3,000, and, according to Bama, a number were sold, including one large Phase II for "a couple of thousand" and one of Bama's own for "a couple of thousand and a half."

The Razor Gallery show attracted the interest of the press, and UGA members were interviewed by television reporters Melba Tolliver and Theresa Brown and a number of newspapers. Press coverage was, in general, positive. Peter Schjeldahl reviewed the show for the *New York Times*: "It is a pleasure to report that respectable standing and the 'art' context have not cowed most of the UGA artists. The show-off ebullience of their work has, if anything been heightened by the comforts of a studio situation. . . . For all their untutored crudities, none of these [canvases] would do discredit to a collection of contemporary art."[8] *Newsweek* reporter S. K. Overbeck also attended the show and reported being entranced by the "wildly expressive works of such graffiti masters as Phase 2, Flint, Mico, Slim 1, T-Rex 131, Tabu, Bama and Me 1263 which send out their carnival message in a caterwauling fantasia of neon superdoodles and shocking-pink stars, stripes and arrows."[9]

After the Razor Gallery show, according to Bama, "we cooled out and got into ourselves as artists." Bama, Wicked Gary, and Co-Co began to sculpt and paint in nongraffiti style because, according to Bama, they were "waking up into the higher art." Apparently Martinez did not wholly approve of all of their efforts. Wicked Gary has said that his first and only painting in nongraffiti style was disapproved of by Martinez, and it was "painted over" without his permission.

Meanwhile Martinez had arranged for the UGA artists to go to Chicago for a showing at the Museum of Science and Industry. He set them to work on graffiti-style canvases, and in the winter of 1974 six of them left to present their art to Chicago. From the start, the trip presented the writers with numerous difficulties. Contrary to their expectations, no one met them when they arrived, and their first five hours in Chicago were spent waiting in the train station. Then they found that space had not been reserved for them, as they had believed, in a first-class hotel across from the museum. Instead they were taken to a YMCA, which, Bama said, "was filled with juveniles and weird people." Once settled they discovered that most of their canvases had been left in New York and had to be sent for.

Publicity photograph for the U.G.A.'s Razor Gallery show. *UGA, Inc.*

Jack Pelsinger poses in front of the first NOGA studio with a painting by Scorpio. *Yolanda Rodriquez*

Because they had to wait for the paintings to be shipped, they had ample time to tour the city. On their first walking venture into the city, Bama said:

We got chased. We were run down the street by an ornery mob of young white people who didn't appreciate young Puerto Ricans and blacks walking in their neighborhood. We said something to some people in a car. Co-Co's the one who said it. They said, "What's that over there? Is that a bunch of niggers? We see a bunch of niggers." And Co-Co said, "No, no, no! I'm Puerto Rican!" . . . And they jumped out of the car with baseball bats and we had to run. But we didn't know where to go. So we split up and started running in strange neighborhoods. . . . We're saying, "Am I running into or out of the fucker?" . . . It was crazy.

The writers generally stayed around the YMCA after that experience until the day before their show was to open, the day their canvases arrived. They stayed up through the night and hung the eighty paintings themselves. They received no help from the museum staff because, according to Bama, "they didn't give us any respect at the museum . . . all they did was hurt us."

After the opening more problems ensued. Martinez arranged for the UGA members to meet with the Blackstone Rangers, a notorious Chicago street gang, hoping that the artists might encourage them to take up graffiti painting. Martinez delivered them to the gang's headquarters and then left. Bama described the atmosphere of the meeting that followed:

We had a great meeting with these dudes, these hoodlums! These massive seventy-five big black boys who were out to kill us. They said, "Y'all from New York, y'all supposed to be bad." Why we were there was because we were supposed to be setting them up with a program . . . where they make a little bit of change and do something constructive. But their idea of something constructive is selling cocaine and getting two bills a week and sitting back on their asses and scaring people. . . . It scared us and made me go home. I got so scared I said, "I'm getting out of here," and I went home.

Three of the six artists left that night with Bama. The rest stayed in Chicago with Martinez for the duration of the show. When they regrouped in New York, Co-Co and Bama decided to "oust Hugo" and to assert themselves as the elected leaders of the group.

Martinez was demoted from director to adviser, and the rules of the organization were changed. The regimented hours and rules of conduct that had applied in the past were abandoned, and members were encouraged to explore new areas of art. The group held a final exhibition at the Artists Space Gallery in SoHo and then, according to Bama:

> The place started to generate for a little while but we were pushing everyone to get into their own thing and that's what led to the group's demise, was the fact that everyone went into their own directions and at the end of '75 it ended . . . it just faded. Someone got involved with his work, someone got involved with school . . . the reason UGA ended was so that we could go on to the next phase of life, our next goals as artists. . . . We can't stay stagnant, we've got to keep moving. . . . Like Co-Co was always talking about all the time: "What are we doing this for? Are we doing it for UGA or are we doing it because we want a message out there?" . . . We decided the message was the most important thing, so that's what happened.

UGA, for all of its problems, appears to have had a positive effect on the lives of a number of its members. The UGA writers grew as artists—not only in their painting skills but in their confidence and sense of being serious artists. Bama said:

> We talked a lot: we talked about what we were going to do. We talked about what we had to do about ourselves. We talked about what we wanted to do, how we had a life. These were things that we were thinking about, we can do things, we're just not little street urchins. We started to realize what we, just us, can do. Because we just got our shit together. Because we had just done a museum show and there are people who wait their whole lives to do a show. It was unreal. We could do whatever we wanted to do if we put our hearts to it.

Of the original twelve members of UGA, eight went to college and four to art schools. Co-Co, who had been flunking out of George Washington High School when he joined UGA, improved his school work and went to study at the School of Visual Arts. Today both he and Bama, who studied at the Pratt Institute of Art, are professional artists. Hugo Martinez also, apparently, saw UGA chiefly as an educational experience: "The group evolved not only as a vehicle by which graffiti artists preserved their art form but also as a place to learn collective leadership, individual motivation and aspirations for higher education. It is within the area of alternative education—alternative both to the schools and the streets—that its history can best be evaluated."[10]

NOGA

Before he got involved with graffiti, Jack Pelsinger had studied acting and ballet; worked the night shift at a freight company; studied painting at the Art Students League in Manhattan; appeared as lead dancer in a nationally touring production of *The Merry Widow*; owned and served as proprietor of a Greenwich Village coffee house; studied dance with Martha Graham; toured the southern part of the country (under the name Jack Spencer) with a nightclub dance act; driven a gypsy cab in Manhattan; worked as an instructor for an Arthur Murray dance studio; performed with the modern dance companies of Alwin Nicholais, Pearl Lang, and Doris Humphrey; directed a number of off-off-Broadway plays (one of his most notable ventures was a multimedia "happening" called *Freak!*); and shot a video documentary on the lives of American Indians in New York City. In 1972 Jack developed an interest in UGA through a visit to their City College exhibition. From that point on he devoted his full attention to graffiti writers and their art.

Jack offered UGA the use of his loft as a studio and meeting place, and with their permission he and Michael Lawrence, a professional photographer, videotaped and photographed many of their activities. Later when UGA moved to its own studio in Washington Heights, he went there frequently, participating in their meetings and other activities. Jack was enthusiastic about the work being done by UGA, and he won the friendship of many of the members, but he did not approve of the organization's exclusive status as a master group nor of what he perceived as Hugo Martinez's "bigoted" attitude toward non-Hispanic members. Jack commented on his feelings toward these matters in an interview: "When I used to see Hugo reject little kids from that workshop—it was terrible. The members of the group were shut off; they weren't learning to reach out to their young brothers and that had to be hurting them. Also, Hugo was racist. He had a quota, a literal quota for black members, and he tried to exclude them from meetings by conducting them mainly in Spanish. The black members were frustrated and they ended up coming to me to talk about their problems."

In summer 1974 Jack decided to start his own organization, one that would be open to all writers and that, he said, "would not take kids out of their communities and into SoHo but would go to a community and grow with it and participate in its life." For help in getting the workshop going, Jack enlisted the aid of a young street artist named Scorpio:

> I used to see Scorpio around my block, on 93d Street. He was always drunk and he slept out there. He had no home. He wore a jacket that had a beautiful design painted on it and that struck me. I finally asked him about it one day and he said that he'd painted it himself; he liked to paint. I invited him to come up to my place to draw. That night he started painting and drawing, and he became totally involved. He stayed at my house and worked continuously for two months.
>
> Meanwhile I talked this community group, the Mid West-Side Community Development Corporation (one of those antipoverty groups that have federal funds), into letting me have the use of a city-owned dollar-a-month storefront that they had over on Columbus Avenue at 88th Street. It took some talking, but they agreed to let us have it, and they'd pay the rent and provide a little bit of money to help us get some supplies.
>
> I told Scorpio about my plan to open the workshop and asked him if he would be my helper. We would do it together. He agreed and for two weeks we did the hard physical labor—knocking down free-standing walls, carting out tons of junk.

He worked even harder than I did, worked constantly. He was completely dedicated to the idea of having a place to work, to learn to draw and paint.

After a while help arrived. Scorpio knew a lot of the kids in the neighborhood, and when they saw him working so diligently they decided that the workshop must be very important. They joined in and painted and cleaned and brought in furniture from the street.

Meanwhile Scorpio built himself a loft in the workshop. He was going to be like the caretaker, keep an eye on things. From then on he was always there, sleeping and working and talking seven days a week.

When the workshop opened in early July 1974, it already had acquired a large membership consisting of those who had helped with the renovation work. At the first meeting of the members they chose Nation of Graffiti Artists (NOGA) as their organization's name. As word spread, writers from other areas of the city joined and participated in NOGA's activities.

Using markers, paint, and other materials, most of which Jack bought, the members set to work. As their artwork improved, they were graduated from markers and paper to paint and canvasboard. Those who showed exceptional talent were given canvases and acrylic paint to use, a particular and expensive privilege, and those so honored made a special effort to use the materials well.

The workshop was very small, about twenty by thirty feet, and was often crowded with fifty or more young people. Someone had donated a conga drum and a rundown piano to the group, and music accompanied their activities continuously. Jack also tried to have food around so that the artists would not be hungry (most of them were poor and in much need of food). When none was otherwise available some of the kids would rack up food for the group, particularly, according to Jack, "when birthdays were celebrated and we needed a cake."

NOGA held its first exhibition that December in the lobby of the Central Savings Bank at 73d Street and Broadway, not far from the workshop. At this time Livi French, an interior designer, graphic artist, and office manager of an East Side art gallery, came into contact with NOGA. Livi had met Jack through UGA; she had attended their exhibitions and had wanted to participate but had been turned down by Hugo Martinez. Livi liked graffiti-style art and believed it had many potential applications, particularly in fabric design, and when she saw an interview with NOGA members on a local news broadcast, she hurried to the bank to meet them. She described her first encounter with NOGA: "I walked into this enormous place, this stodgy quiet bank and here were a bunch of kids lying around on the floor under their paintings, bored. Some were sleeping. Then Jack walked in very quietly waving a newspaper and said in a loud voice: 'Up! Everybody up!' They gathered around him and he read them an article in the *New York Post*, NOGA's first publicity. They were ecstatic, they cheered at the best parts."[11] Livi promptly joined the organization and was quickly declared NOGA's business manager and public-relations expert, a position she still holds.

NOGA expanded quickly that winter, and among its members it counted some of the city's more accomplished writers, including Cliff 159, Stan 153, IN, OZ, Chino Malo, Rib 161, and Kase. Most of the members, however, were lesser-known writers and children from the surrounding area, who were too young to have begun writing on trains, who went to the workshop to socialize with the writers and learn to paint and draw.

Jack and Livi have described some of NOGA's key members:

Livi:

Tony was shaved absolutely bald—he looked like a wild man—he always carried a machete and talked about all sorts of strange West Indian superstitions.

Jack:

But he used to walk me home every night—take care of me so I shouldn't get mugged.

Livi:

Blood Tea. He was everywhere; he lived in the workshop. He's a very talented artist and loved to work with other kids—a natural leader. When I first arrived at the workshop he hated me—we joke about this now—his appearance couldn't scare a flea, he's such a cute kid. But he was giving me these dagger looks.

Jack:

He thought you were a narc. He had been a gang member, a Young Nomad before he joined NOGA. They taught him that white people usually were cops—anybody white who walked into the workshop got a careful once-over from a lot of the kids.

Livi:

Spooky seemed like a really sweet kid—he had this pink cherubic face. Later I found out he had this fascination with knives and guns and pornography. He had a vast collection of pornography. He used to ask people to call him "the prince of darkness." He could paint though.

Jack:

RB had some real problems. He couldn't do simple math. He'd bring in his books and Blood Tea and I would work with him for hours, but he could not learn his multiplication tables. And he wanted to be an accountant—had his heart set on it. He coped with life by painting. He'd work all night, reworking everything, going over his paintings until he felt they were perfect. His work was beautiful.

Livi:

Do It. We found him on the doorstep, literally passed out on the doorstep, drunk.

Jack:

We brought him into the workshop and put him on a table—let him sleep it off. When he got up he saw all of the paintings . . . he was fascinated. He stayed.

Livi:

He had never been a graffiti artist. He had done some drawing in prison but had never been to the trains. He wanted to learn to be a graffiti artist and the other kids taught him. He was twenty-six and fourteen year olds were his mentors. He would listen to them for hours, go out painting with them. He worked out a style with their help and advice. He needed a name so he chose Zero. The other kids didn't like it—too negative—so they started calling him Do It. They got it from Jack who was always after him to keep painting, saying "Do it, get to work—paint— do it!"

Throughout 1975 NOGA exhibited and occasionally sold canvases at a variety of street fairs and festivals around the city. NOGA's members also began to participate in activities other than painting. Jack explained, "I wanted to get the kids involved in everything. I took them to museums, readings, free concerts, meetings, demonstrations. I once took eighty-eight NOGA kids down to Washington for a protest. I also had them out in our neighborhood, knocking on doors with all sorts of petitions. They were getting into the life of the community." On March 3, 1976, NOGA held its first (and only, to date) large exhibition at the Bank Street College of Education. Paintings by twenty-five NOGA artists were displayed, and a table was set up nearby where members drew customers' names for them in graffiti style on small canvas boards for $5 each. A few large canvases were sold, some for as much as $300, and the artists split their fees seventy-five—twenty-five with the organization.

In spite of the sales at the Bank Street show and a small grant from the Western Electric Company, NOGA continued to lack funds. Materials were perpetually in short supply, and a number of members left the organization to go back to full-time painting because, in Blood Tea's words, "in the yards, at least they had something to paint on."

In September 1976 NOGA was offered an opportunity to paint a mural at Prospect Hospital in the Bronx. Jack accepted, feeling sure that the fee for the work, though an amount was never discussed, might help to hold NOGA together. On the appointed day Jack and twelve NOGA members arrived at Prospect Hospital. The hospital supplied spray paint and an enormous sheet canvas, and the artists set to work in an empty lot next door to the hospital. The mural painting became, as NOGA always preferred, a community event. Blood Tea played the conga, and a crowd gathered to hear the music and watch the progress of the painting. Children from the neighborhood, one of the poorest in New York, were encouraged to take part in the activity.

When the mural was complete, Jacob Freedman, director and owner of the hospital, thanked the artists and had the mural rolled and taken into the hospital. He then started back to his office. At that point, Jack related, "I asked him for the money. 'What money?' he said. 'The money for the artists!' He acted like he didn't understand. It was like he was saying, 'What! Pay kids for painting a mural for my hospital!' Well, I kept after him and finally he coughed up a hundred dollars. A hundred dollars for a mural that had taken all day to complete." The hundred dollars was divided among the artists; it came to a little over seven dollars each. The artists were so delighted with the mural that they hardly seemed to mind the fact that their fee was very small. They were, however, profoundly disappointed that the work was rolled and stored in the hospital basement rather than displayed where the public could see and enjoy it.

In fall 1976 the New York Housing and Development Agency evicted NOGA from its workshop. New York was in the midst of a budget problem, and rents on all city property were raised to $55 a month. The community development group that had been paying NOGA's dollar-a-month rent refused to cover this increase. NOGA was unable to raise the necessary funds itself and so, on October 10, 1976, the NOGA workshop closed and all of the paintings and materials were moved to Jack's apartment. One week later city workers whitewashed and sealed the storefront, which has remained vacant since.

Some of the members continued to meet and work at Jack's house. One of their projects was a proposal to the MTA. Blood Tea had managed to obtain a number of blueprints of subway cars, and he, Scorpio, and Cliff filled them in with colorful designs. Their plan was to convince transit officials to allow them to paint their proposed designs on ten subway cars. They reasoned that since the MTA was said to spend $1,500 per car to paint a car themselves, a fee of $150 per car would be their price and the money would be used to start a new workshop. Jack liked the idea and went with them to present the idea at the MTA's headquarters in Brooklyn, but they were turned down.

In 1977 a Methodist church in the South Bronx made part of its basement, and later a nearby storefront, available to NOGA. Since that time the organization has grown. It now has about fifty young members, including the former president and nine other members of the Savage Nomads. Blood Tea and Jack commute to the Bronx workshop five days a week and keep it open from noon until eight P.M. Funding for materials remains scant. Some money has been acquired from the

New York State Council on the Arts, and the group has received a small amount, for painting a mural, from Montefiore Hospital, but as Jack says, "It's not enough; it's never enough. We need paint and canvas and we don't have them. We need food; these kids are hungry. If we had the money, there is so much that we could do. These kids respond instantly to new materials. They would love to work with clay. They should be able to do silkscreening and photography. Everybody has the need to be someone—to feel important and be important to others. Art is the quickest way to do that and these kids need it. Why can't those bureaucrats who have control over all the money see that?"

Livi French has said of Jack and NOGA's many problems, "Jack has probably missed some chances for funding because he isn't much of a negotiator. He hates dealing with the people downtown. He'd just rather be with the kids. Struggling for funding has been hard for him; he's had to devote a lot of time to it, but he can't stand it. It's funny; for five years he's been telling me, 'I'm fed up. One more year and then I give up.' But he can't seem to quit." Jack has speculated on NOGA's future and his part in it: "Sometimes I wake up and I think, 'I'm nuts. What am I doing this for?' Then I go up and I see the kids and I know. I know. I've been thinking about leaving New York, maybe go to Jamaica, and write a book about all of this. I'll give NOGA another year, though. I'll stick with it for just one more year."

7

The Politics
of Graffiti

Henry Chalfant

In 1972 subway graffiti became a political issue in New York City. In that year and the two following, a variety of elected and appointed city officials, particularly Mayor John V. Lindsay, devised and debated graffiti-related policies and programs and issued numerous public statements on the subject.

In examining the progress of subway graffiti as a political issue, New York's newspapers and magazines serve as a revealing and important resource, for not only did they report the graffiti policies of public officials but seemingly played a role in motivating and shaping them as well.

By summer 1971 the appearance of the mysterious message "Taki 183" had sufficiently aroused the curiosity of New Yorkers to lead the *New York Times* to send one of its reporters to determine its meaning. The results of his search, published on July 21, 1971, revealed that Taki was an unemployed seventeen year old with nothing better to do than pass the summer days spraying his name wherever he happened to be. He explained, "I just did it everywhere I went. I still do, though not as much. You don't do it for girls; they don't seem to care. You do it for yourself. You don't go after it to be elected president."[2] The reporter interviewed other neighborhood youths, including Julio 204 and Ray A.O. (for "all over"), who were following in the footsteps of Taki, to whom they referred as the king, and he spoke with an official of the MTA who stated that more than $300,000 was being spent annually to erase graffiti. Patrolman Floyd Holoway, a vice-president of the Transit Patrolmen's Benevolent Association questioned by the reporter as to the legal machinery relating to graffiti writing, explained that graffiti was barred only by MTA rules, not by law. Thus writers under the age of sixteen could only be given a lecture, not a summons, even if they were caught in the act of writing on the walls. Adult writers could be charged with malicious mischief and sentenced to up to a year's imprisonment.

Taki confessed that as he grew older, he worried more about facing adult penalties for writing graffiti but admitted, "I could never retire . . . besides . . . it doesn't harm anybody. I work, I pay taxes too. Why do they go after the little guy? Why not the campaign organizations that put stickers all over the subways at election time?"[3]

The *Times* article presented Taki as an engaging character with a unique and fascinating hobby, and this seemed to have a profound effect on the city's youth. Taki became something of a folk hero, and the ranks of the graffiti writers increased enormously. However, though each day brought numerous new writers to the walls and the subways were marked with names from top to bottom, 1971 brought no further press coverage of graffiti.

In spring 1972 another article on graffiti appeared in the press. It was intended not to help familiarize New Yorkers with the writers but to declare war on them. On May 21 city council president Sanford Garelik told reporters, "Graffiti pollutes the eye and mind and may be one of the worst forms of pollution we have to combat." He called upon the citizens of New York to band together and wage "an all-out war on graffiti" and recommended the establishment of a monthly "antigraffiti day" on which New Yorkers, under the auspices of the Environmental Protection Agency, would scrub walls, fences, public buildings, subway stations, and subway cars.[4]

The *Times*'s management followed up on Garelik's statement by printing an editorial denouncing the "wanton use of spray paint to deface subways." They praised Garelik's "noble concept" of an antigraffiti day but questioned its lasting appeal. Rather than burden the populace with the responsibility for cleaning up graffiti, the *Times* called upon the city administration to ban the sale of spray paint to minors and thus stop graffiti at its source.[5]

Taking his cue from both the *Times*'s and Garelik's suggestions, Mayor Lindsay announced his own antigraffiti program in late June. The mayor's proposal called for the fining and jailing of anyone caught with an open spray can in any municipal building or facility. Lindsay was highly agitated at the time of the announcement, and Robert Laird, his assistant press secretary, admitted to a *Times* reporter that "the unsightly appearance of the subways and other public places created by the so-called graffiti artists has disturbed the Mayor greatly."[6]

Lindsay again addressed the graffiti problem in extemporaneous comments before a large crowd at the rededication ceremonies for Brooklyn's Prospect Park boathouse in late August. Standing before the white ceramic exterior of the newly renovated structure, Lindsay noted that he had asked for tighter legislation against graffiti vandalism but said that police action alone would not cure the problem. Pleading for greater public interest in the problem, the mayor exclaimed, "For heaven's sake, New Yorkers, come to the aid of your great city—defend it, support it and protect it!"[7]

Lindsay's graffiti legislation had been referred to the city council's General Welfare Committee in early August, but the members had shown little inclination to deal with it at that time. (The council meets only twice during the summer months, and committee activity is virtually suspended from July to September.) Impatient with the committee's foot dragging, Lindsay insisted that they hold a special meeting on graffiti on August 31. The mayor asked a number of top administration officials, including the deputy mayor, the parks commissioner, and the MTA chief administrator, to testify in favor of the legislation. But only four members of the fifteen-member committee were present at the session, and no action was immediately forthcoming.[8]

Meanwhile MTA chairman Ronan publicly gave his support to Mayor Lindsay's graffiti campaign. On October 28 he told reporters that he had instructed the transit police to charge "such miscreants with 'malicious mischief,'" and he urged the mayor to stress the seriousness of "this blighting epidemic" to the courts.[9] Later that same day Mayor Lindsay held a ceremony in his office at which he officially commended one of Dr. Ronan's transit policemen, patrolman Steven Schwartz, for his "personal crusade" against graffiti. Schwartz alone had apprehended thirteen writers in the previous six months, a record for graffiti arrests unmatched in the department. The mayor followed up the ceremony with a statement that it was the "Lindsay theory" that graffiti writing "is related to mental health problems." He described the writers as "insecure cowards" seeking recognition.[10]

The General Welfare Committee submitted a graffiti bill to the city council in mid-September stating that the use of markers and spray paint to write graffiti has "reached proportions requiring serious punishment for the perpetrators" and that such defacement and the use of "foul language" in many of the writings is "harmful to the general public and violative of the good and welfare of the people of the city of New York."[11] The bill proposed to eliminate graffiti by making it illegal to carry an aerosol can of paint into a public facility "unless it is completely enclosed in a sealed container." It specified that "no person shall write, paint or draw any inscription, figure or mark of any type" on any public property. Judges were given wide latitude in dealing with such offenses, but the law stated that it was the council's intent that any person guilty of writing graffiti "should be punished so that the punishment shall fit the crime." In this spirit the bill recommended that judges sentence writers "to remove graffiti under the supervision of an employee of the public works office, New York City transit authority or other officer or employee designated by the court."[12] The bill also recommended that merchants selling spray paint or markers be required to register with the Police Department and to keep a record of the names and addresses of all persons who purchase such merchandise.[13]

The day after the General Welfare Committee approved the bill, the *Times* published an editorial stating that graffiti "are day-glo bright and multicolored, sometimes obscene, always offensive." The editorial praised the committee for getting tough with "youthful vandals" and announced that "graffiti are no longer amusing; they have become a public menace."[14]

Perhaps intending to spur the full council on to faster action on the graffiti law, Mayor Lindsay on October 5 announced the formation of a graffiti task force under the direction of his chief of staff, Steven Isenberg. The task force, which included among its members the heads of a number of city agencies, was designed to coordinate "tough new programs" for the enforcement of the expected graffiti legislation.[15] The mayor further stated that "the ugliness of graffiti and the ugly message—often obscene or racist—has generated widespread support for the City's campaign to end this epidemic of thoughtless behavior. Even those who once possessed mild amusement about graffiti are becoming increasingly indignant at the damage being done. . . . I know the problem is complex, but we have to roll up our sleeves and solve it. The assault on our senses and on our pocketbooks as we pay the clean-up costs must be stopped."[16]

The graffiti bill was approved unanimously by the full city council on October 11, minus the section on control of the sale of spray paint, which had aroused opposition from merchants and was considered by the council to be "too controversial."[17]

Mayor Lindsay, who signed it into law on October 27, was pleased with the bill but warned merchants to "self-regulate" their sales or he would impose further legislation that would make it illegal to sell spray paint to anyone under eighteen years of age.[18]

There was also antigraffiti action on other fronts. Science came to the aid of graffiti fighters with the invention, by E. Dragza of the Samson Chemical Corporation, of an "artproof acrylic polymer hydron" which he named Dirty Word Remover (DWR).[19] On July 31 Mayor Lindsay announced that Dragza's formula, renamed Hydron 300, was to be sprayed on a library in Queens, another in Brooklyn, and a firehouse in the Bronx, to facilitate the removal of graffiti from their walls. The Mayor expressed hopes that use of the "Teflon-like coating" would help to make graffiti removal "easier and less costly." The cost of the experiment was set at $5,000.[20] Results of the test were never made public.

Inspired by the growing campaign against graffiti, private citizens also got involved in the "graffiti war" of 1972. In November the Kings County Council of Jewish War Veterans invited "citizens of good will" to join their bucket brigade to clean graffiti off the monument to President John F. Kennedy in Brooklyn's Grand Army Plaza.[21] The Boy Scouts and Girl Scouts staged their own graffiti cleanup day when more than 400 scouts spent a day partially cleaning six IND trains. Each participating scout received a citizenship medallion in honor of his or her achievement from the Avon Products Corporation.[22]

Other New Yorkers devised ingenious solutions to the problem. E. A. Sachs, for example, in a letter to the *New York Times* suggested that the MTA paint subway vehicles with a "multi-colored spray" that would "camouflage any attempts at graffiting."[23] M. W. Covington, also in a letter, made the more drastic suggestion that a "massive police assault" be launched against graffitists who deface Central Park monuments.[24] R. H. Robinson of Brooklyn showed great ingenuity in his suggestion that large fines levied on convicted graffitists be divided between the city and persons turning in the graffitists. He noted that he had already assembled a lengthy list of offenders in his own neighborhood.[25] Of more than a dozen letters concerning graffiti that appeared in the *Times* that winter, only one was sympathetic to the writers. The letter writer, P. R. Patterson, hailed youths who paint graffiti for "cheering up the depressing environment in the poorer areas of the city" and accused most people of being "guilty of subduing the desire to mark up subways as a protest against the indignities of the city bureaucracy."[26]

Early in 1973 Steven Isenberg announced that over the year the police had arrested 1,562 youths for defacing subways and other public places with graffiti. Of those arrested, 426 eventually went to court and were sentenced to spend a day in the train yards scrubbing graffiti.[27]

Two weeks after Isenberg's announcement Frank Berry, the executive officer of the transit authority, announced that conventional "quick treatment" graffiti writing had reached the "saturation level" and was being supplanted by "large . . . multi-colored inscriptions that may cover one-half or more of a subway car's outer surface." The alarming proliferation of such "grand design" graffiti constituted, according to Berry, distinct danger to riders because "they can block the vision of riders preparing to enter or leave through the door." In light of these new developments Berry called for an increase in the number of graffiti arrests to eliminate the possibility of a "grand design" epidemic.[28]

On February 26 the New York City Bureau of the Budget completed a detailed work plan for Mayor Lindsay's graffiti task force. The report began by stating that antigraffiti efforts in 1972 had cost the city $10 million, yet they had not been sufficient to reduce "the city-wide level of graffiti defacement" below "fifty percent surface coverage," a level that it declared "unacceptable."[29] It thus proposed that the city engage in a graffiti prevention project that would seek to reduce the level of defacement to an acceptable 10 to 20 percent. The cost of such a project was estimated to be $24 million.[30]

Under the control of a project management staff team appointed by the mayor, the proposed project would coordinate efforts by various city agencies and private corporations toward four major project elements:

- Technological improvements: Testing and implementing the use of high-performance paints, coatings, and solvents for graffiti-defaced surfaces.
- Security measures: Testing and implementing increased

security measures in those areas of the city where security may deter graffiti vandalism.

- Motivation of graffiti vandals: Testing and implementing psychological measures aimed at either inhibiting vandalism or diverting vandals elsewhere.

- Control of graffiti instruments: Testing and implementing the feasibility of manufacturer and retailer restrictions on packaging and display of graffiti instruments.[31]

Under these categories the report listed nearly one hundred specific tasks, the completion of which would lead to the achievement of the overall objectives. The tasks included "implementing and monitoring psychological field-testing for graffiti vandalism prevention and developing procedures for monitoring of procedures involved in implementation of restrictions." Mayor Lindsay devoted a month to study of the report before releasing it or commenting on it publicly.

Meanwhile on March 26 *New York Magazine* published a long article by Richard Goldstein, "This Thing Has Gotten Completely Out of Hand." His reference was not to the growing graffiti fad but to the city's fight against it. Goldstein, giving the pro-graffiti forces their first published support, stated that "it just may be that the kids who write graffiti are the healthiest and most assertive people in their neighborhoods." He further declared graffiti to be "the first genuine teenage street culture since the fifties. In that sense, it's a lot like rock 'n' roll."[32]

In the same issue the *New York Magazine* management presented a "Graffiti 'Hit' Parade" in which it gave "Taki awards" to a number of graffitists in categories labeled "Grand Design" and "Station Saturation." Award-winning works were reproduced in full color in the magazine. They declared the emergence of grand design pieces a "grand graffiti conquest of the subways" and ridiculed chairman Ronan, Mayor Lindsay, and the *Times* for their attitude toward the new art form. The Taki Awards article also contained a statement in praise of graffiti from pop artist Claes Oldenberg that was reprinted in the catalog for two subsequent UGA exhibitions and was quoted in a number of magazine and newspaper articles about graffiti, as well as Norman Mailer's book, *The Faith of Graffiti*. Said Oldenberg:

I've always wanted to put a steel band with dancing girls in the subways and send it all over the city. It would slide into a station without your expecting it. It's almost like that now. You're standing there in the station, everything is gray and gloomy and all of a sudden one of those graffiti trains slides in and brightens the place like a big bouquet from Latin America. At first it seems anarchical—makes you wonder if the subways are working properly. Then you get used to it. The city is like a newspaper anyway, so it's natural to see writing all over the place.[33]

The day after the *New York* articles appeared, Mayor Lindsay called a press conference at which he discussed the findings and proposals contained in the graffiti prevention project report. He stated that copies of the work plan would be sent to the heads of the MTA, the Environmental Protection Agency, the board of education, and all other agencies and authorities concerned with graffiti prevention. He ridiculed "those who call graffiti vandalism 'art'" and asked the citizens of New York to join him in denouncing the graffiti vandals. "It's a dirty shame," said the mayor, "that we must spend money for this purpose in a time of austerity. The cost of cleaning up graffiti, even to a partial extent, is sad testimony to the impact of the thoughtless behavior which lies behind . . . the demoralizing visual impact of graffiti."[34]

As graffiti continued to appear on subways and other city property, Mayor Lindsay became increasingly angry, not only at supporters of graffiti and the writers themselves but at his own staff for their inability to control the problem. In an interview with a *Sunday News* reporter, Steven Isenberg "smiled when he recalled two times when Mayor Lindsay burst into his office and—with four-letter fervor—ordered him to 'clean up the mess.' One time the Mayor had snipped a ceremonial ribbon at the opening of a Brooklyn swimming pool that was already covered with graffiti and the other time he had spotted a graffiti-laden bus in midtown. 'I certainly got reamed out,' Isenberg recalled."[35]

The mayor's anger over the continued appearance of graffiti on the subways exploded publicly on June 30, 1973. Steven Isenberg explained, "When the Mayor went to midtown to publicize the parking ticket step-up, he took the subway back to City Hall and what he saw made him madder than hell."[36] Immediately upon his return to his office the mayor called a hurried press conference at which he snapped, "I just came back from 42nd Street in one of [MTA chairman] Dr. Ronan's graffiti-scarred subway cars, one of the worst I've seen yet."[37] The mayor stated that the extent of name marking in the trains and stations was "shocking" and pointed out that the antigraffiti force he had organized the year before had come up with a plan to prevent the writing through increased police surveillance of lay-ups, train yards, and stations. "Since the time the plan was sent to the MTA I haven't heard a word," he said. "I don't think they even bothered to look at it. They don't give a damn and couldn't care less about being responsive to elected officials."[38]

A few months later in an interview with Norman Mailer, Lindsay explained that his aggravation with graffiti was due to the fact that it tended to nullify many of his efforts to provide the city's subway passengers with "a cleaner and more pleasant environment" in which to travel. At that time the mayor was also attempting to justify the city's massive expenditures for new subway cars, which, once covered with graffiti, "did not seem much more pleasant" than the old cars.[39]

The graffiti policies that were established during the Lindsay administration are still being pursued. The MTA continues to scrub trains only to find them immediately redecorated. The police continue to apprehend writers only to see them released, unpunished, by the courts. It would seem that the failure of the city's expensive antigraffiti policies should be a matter of great concern to the press and elected officials; however, the management, expense, and overall wisdom of New York City's antigraffiti policies have not been criticized publicly by either politicians or the press and thus continue unchanged.

Norman Mailer attributed Lindsay's attitude toward graffiti to the fact that the mayor had earlier sought the Democratic presidential nomination in 1972 and that graffiti had been "an upset to his fortunes, . . . a vermin of catastrophe that these writings had sprouted like weeds over the misery of Fun City, a new monkey of unmanageables to sit on Lindsay's overloaded political back. He must have sensed the Presidency draining away from him as the months went by, the graffiti grew, and the millions of tourists who passed through the city brought the word out to the rest of the nation: 'Filth is sprouting on the walls.' "[40]

It is doubtful that graffiti played as important a role in Lindsay's declining political fortunes as Mailer speculates. Evidently, however, Lindsay believed that graffiti was a problem significant enough to rate a substantial amount of his attention, and thus it became a political issue during his administration.

The fact that there has been very little reduction in the amount of graffiti that has covered the city's subways since 1971 can be seen as proof that the city's antigraffiti policies have failed. John deRoos, former senior executive director of the MTA, has placed the burden of blame for this failure on the city's judicial system: "Almost all graffiti can be traced to people who have been arrested at least once. But the courts let them off. Six, seven, eight, or nine times."[41] In an interview former transit police chief Sanford Garelik also laid the blame for the failure of the MTA's graffiti arrest policies on the courts: "The transit police are doing their job but what's the use of making arrests if the courts refuse to prosecute? Graffiti is a form of behavior that leads to other forms of criminality. The courts have to realize this . . . anything else is an injustice to the public."

Chief Judge Reginald Matthews of the Bronx Family Court has replied to such criticism of the courts' handling of graffiti: "Graffiti is an expression of social maladjustment, but the courts cannot cure all of society's ills. We have neither the time nor the facilities to handle graffiti cases; in fact, we cannot always give adequate treatment to far more serious crimes. Graffiti simply cannot be treated by the juvenile justice system as a serious thing, not in New York."

Not everyone in the MTA and the transit police blames the courts. Reginal Lewis, a car maintenance foreman at the MTA, puts the blame on the transit police for "not keeping the kids out of the (train) yards." Detective sergeant Morris Bitchachi, commander of the MTA's ten-member graffiti squad, blamed the city's Department of Social Services for not providing special rehabilitation programs for "known graffiti offenders."

City University professor George Jochnowitz had another idea: "The *New York Times* is . . . responsible for the preva-

Attack dogs on patrol at the Corona train yard.

lence of graffiti. On July 21, 1971, an interview with Taki 183, a previously unknown graffiti dauber, appeared. . . . The glorification of this vandal by the nation's most prestigious newspaper was not without effect. Within months a minor problem became a major one."[42]

After 1975 there was little press coverage of graffiti, a reflection of the city government's reluctance to publicize the city's continuing failure to control the graffiti phenomenon. This, combined with the seeming unwillingness of the press to bring criticism upon itself through the publication of other Taki-style reports, led to a near press blackout on the subject of graffiti.

In 1980 the blackout ended when the *New York Times Magazine* published a long article about three graffiti writers: NE, T-Kid, and Seen. Other newspapers followed suit, featuring articles on other writers and on the current state of the graffiti phenomenon.

In September 1981 the mayor's office broke its silence when Mayor Koch declared that, "New Yorkers are fed up with graffiti," and announced a 1.5 million dollar program to provide fences and German Shepherd watchdogs for the Corona trainyard. MTA chairman Richard Ravitch had at first rejected the idea, stating that, "fences are not going to work. It is likely that they would be cut and the dogs would get out and perhaps injure someone in the neighboring community."[43] Ravitch quickly gave in to pressure from the mayor, however, and a double set of razor wire-topped fences were quickly installed, between which six dogs patrolled the perimeter of the yard. Mayor Koch and the press were present on the day the dogs were released and the mayor declared, "We call them dogs, but they are really wolves. Our hope is that the vandals will ultimately get the message."[44]

To test the effectiveness of the fences and dogs, all of the trains stored at the yard were painted white and the mayor asked the MTA to inform him immediately if any graffiti was painted on them. For the following three months the trains were watched closely and no graffiti appeared on the outsides of the trains. Declaring the Corona experiment a success, the mayor announced on December 14 that the city would increase its contribution to the MTA by $22.4 million to fund the installation of similar fences at the other eighteen train yards operated by the authority. The mayor stated that the new security installations would not feature attack dogs because, at $3000 per year apiece, their maintenance had proved too expensive. Instead, coils of razor wire would be placed between the fences. Said Koch, "I prefer to think of these as steel dogs with razor teeth. And you don't have to feed steel dogs."[45] Ravitch said that he was pleased by the mayor's decision to increase transit financing and that the MTA would attempt to complete construction of the new fences within six months.

Privately, MTA officials expressed doubts that the fences would, ultimately, be effective. Graffiti writers did so as well. Said Ali, "We haven't gone over the fences at Corona because it's on a lousy subway line. If they fence a popular yard like Pelham or Coney Island, the writers won't be stopped by razor wire, dogs, or laser towers. We'll get past the fences. Wait and see." Daze said, "All the fences will do is keep most of us out of the yards. We'll still be able to hit the trains in the lay-ups, and we'll bomb the insides and the outsides of in-service trains with tags—big spray-paint tags like nobody's ever seen. The MTA can't stop us from doing that unless they put a cop on every car." Bloodtea continued, "All they're doing is moving graffiti from the outsides of the trains to the insides. It's the inside graffiti—the tags—that the public hates. All the mayor is doing is getting rid of the outside pieces that the public likes, the big colorful pieces."

According to mayoral aide Jack Lusk, the yard-fencing program is the first step in a long-range antigraffiti program. Said Lusk; "The public hates graffiti and it's up to us to do something about it. Fencing the yards will take care of some of it. Beyond that we're planning a series of antigraffiti television, radio, and print advertisements featuring the slogan, 'Make your mark in society, not on it.' We're also considering sponsoring antigraffiti citizens' groups; legislation banning the sale of spray paint and markers to minors; and possibly the establishment of a special transit court that will handle crimes like graffiti and other forms of vandalism. Even though the mayor does not have direct authority over the MTA, the public holds him responsible for the state of the subways. The public is frightened and disgusted by graffiti and they want us to do something about it. We're going to do whatever is necessary to wipe it out."

8

The MTA

The Metropolitan Transit Authority is a state-controlled agency that operates and maintains New York City's public transportation system, which consists in part of more than 700 miles of track, 475 subway stations, 12 storage and maintenance yards, hundreds of lay-up sites, and a rolling stock of nearly 7,000 subway cars. Since the late 1960s when widespread graffiti first began to appear on subway trains, the MTA has devoted a steadily growing amount of effort and increasingly large portions of its budget to graffiti removal.

Graffiti removal has been difficult and expensive for the MTA. Throughout the years 1970 to 1974 subway cars were cleaned by hand with solvents designed to remove only dirt and grime, not paint. In order to eradicate graffiti, MTA employees had to sand and repaint trains, a job that required four days of out-of-service time per car in the maintenance barns, the efforts of more than twenty workers, and $1,800 worth of labor and paint, an amount that was, "equivalent to the revenue from [the sale of] 6,000 tokens."[1]

The clean-up process was slow and expensive, its costs consisting not only of those of actual cleaning but also of "the unquantifiable expenses resulting from frequent disruptions of services to the public during graffiti removal."[2] It also simply did not work. Cars that were painstakingly cleaned and repainted were returned to the tracks only to be almost immediately covered again.

Meanwhile the amount of graffiti written on the trains and the cost of cleaning it off rose steadily. In 1970 the MTA's graffiti-cleaning costs were estimated to be $300,000;[3] in 1971, $600,000;[4] in 1972, $1.3 million;[5] and in 1973, $2.7 million, with "unsatisfactory results."[6]

An experiment with a new cleaning solvent was unsuccessful. Every car in the subway system was scrubbed by hand with a newly developed acid-based cleaner (at a total cost of $4 million) in late fall 1973. "What you see on the cars now has been put there since," said Frank Berry, the MTA's chief operations and maintenance officer, "The trains were almost immediately re-covered with graffiti."[7] In an earlier interview Berry had despaired, "If I have to redo it and redo it, eventually this [solvent] will take off the paint and it costs $3,000 to repaint one car . . . what the hell are you gonna do?"[8]

Not everyone despaired. Newly appointed MTA chairman David Yunich announced, on July 30, 1974, a "ten million dollar program of graffiti eradication," which he called "the most ambitious yet."[9] A key part of his plan was to use attack dogs, then in training: "In the Mosholu yards of the upper Bronx . . . the first two dogs are going through their paces, learning to dodge the third rail. At a brisk command in German ('Fass!' which translates into 'Fetch' or better, 'Get him!') they spring into action sinking their teeth into the padded arm shields worn by their handlers."[10] Yunich expressed some regret that the MTA was forced to take violent action against graffitists but noted that conventional efforts to protect the trains had failed. "They're breaking through fences that ought to be strong enough to stop a bulldozer," said Yunich, "and they're going right down into the tunnels too."[11]

Reports of the viciousness of Yunich's attack dogs moved the *Times* management to abandon temporarily its former antigraffiti stance, now scorning "dour New Yorkers who are offended by subway graffiti." The editorial suggested that MTA money could be better spent hiring more transit police to catch muggers and producing readable subway maps, actions that would raise the level of subway service "to the equivalent of that in Baghdad or Kabul." The article remarked that the MTA planned to raise the cost of tokens fifteen cents and that the money saved by cancelling the new program could be used to postpone the rate hike for nearly a year. "But above all they want to be rid of technicolor information—always striking, sometimes cheerful—on the street-gang affiliations of Juan III and his colleagues in art. The MTA may be slow to act but it sure does know its priorities."[12] This was a large change of sentiment by a newspaper whose previous graffiti editorials typified graffitists as "animals," "youthful vandals," and "a public menace." The *Times* also provided space on its editorial page for a number of letters scoring the MTA's dog program.

Meanwhile Yunich told a *Daily News* reporter that he was "very, very fearful of adverse public reaction but unless we get rid of the graffiti on the cars, it's no use telling the passenger he is going to have a clean ride."[13]

Under the provisions of the new graffiti law, the transit police arrested and charged increasing numbers of writers. In

1973 and the first three months of 1974, 2,525 were charged under the law and 774 of them were assigned to clean-up details by the courts.[14] In spite of the arrests, the amount of graffiti being written on the trains did not decrease. In April 1974 Frank Berry stated, "The graffiti law has proved no deterrent whatsoever. . . . On weekends the kids who have been found guilty scrub down cars and stations . . . but to them it's a lark and mainly an opportunity to exchange notes. The cleaned spaces just provide a new surface to work on the next week."[15]

On August 6 a second test of the guard dogs was held at the Concourse yards in the upper Bronx. Yunich and reporters attended, this time watching as a "Rottweiler named Missy and a German shepherd named Thunder held an actor pretending to be a graffiti artist at bay with barks and snarls."[16] Yunich emphasized that the MTA now planned only to "use the dogs' natural sensitivities . . . to help human guards locate the intruders" and that the dogs would attack only in defense of their handlers.[17] Yunich also noted that the MTA had received much criticism since its earlier announcement regarding the guard dogs, and he assured reporters that "we are only in the very preliminary stages and we hope to find out if using dogs will be feasible."[18]

Shortly after a top transit official was quoted in the *Daily News* as saying, "The dogs won't help. Containing the thing [graffiti] is like trying to stop a rolling fog."[19] Three months after the dog tests, the *New York Times* noted that a call to the MTA had elicited the information that "following the demonstration last summer the guard dogs were dropped. The Chairman was not impressed."[20]

In March 1975 a highly publicized report from the office of state controller Robert Levitt criticized the transit authority for "its ineffective and costly handling of the graffiti problem."[21] Chairman Yunich responded that graffiti "is a sociological problem that has defied solution" and that a "cutback in resources allocated to graffiti control will be immediately effected."[22] MTA senior executive officer John deRoos confirmed later that summer that a cutback in graffiti cleaning was taking place. He noted that "several campaigns against grafitti" had failed and stated that "such crackdowns are no longer a top priority."[23]

DeRoos went on to lay the blame for the continuing "graffiti menace" on "lenient judges" and press coverage that "makes the culprits appear like heroes." He also admitted that "what we found out in cleaning the trains was that we were providing the vandals with a clean slate and they were putting the graffiti right back on." The *Times* summed all of this up by stating that a "youthful army of graffiti commandoes, estimated at no more than 400, has not only painted scrawls on nearly all of the 6700 subway cars, it has also painted the Transit Authority into a corner."[24]

Finally in May 1976 John deRoos announced, "We think we have finally come up with a practical solution to the graffiti problem."[25] The solution was a polyurethane-based paint developed over two years of experimentation by MTA chemists, representatives of five paint manufacturers, and consultants from the National Aeronautics and Space Administration who had "substantial experience in the creation of coating materials with unusual properties."[26] The most important property of the new paint was the resistance to strong graffitti-removing solvents. Jamaica (Queens) yard superintendent Tom Pope explained, "Before, the kids were using better paint than ours. The solvent took off our paint easier than theirs. Not any more . . . we're ahead of the graffitti kids now."[27]

The MTA executive officer for rapid transit, Steven Kaufman, stated that by 1980 all 3,600 of the authority's painted (non-stainless steel) cars would be coated with the new substance.[28] John deRoos estimated the cost of the repainting effort at $9 million.[29] He also noted that new and more powerful solvents were needed to remove graffiti efficiently but stated that "hopefully by next spring we will have developed such a solvent."[30]

It took until October 1977 to develop a solvent that would both remove graffiti and could be used efficiently in the MTA's new "train-wash machines" (open-air automated machines very much like those used by commercial car washers). The transit authority demonstrated the new solvent for the press at the Jamaica yards, thoroughly cleaning a train that had been written on with white paint by transit workers by running it through the machines twice. The cost of a single washing with the new solvent was given as $80 per car.[31] Authority

*"Graffiti-wash machine" at the Coney
Island train yard.* Ted Pearlman

*A typical "scrubbed" car,
photographed just after a trip through
the graffiti-wash machine.*
Ted Pearlman

representatives stated that they planned to run all 7,000 subway cars through the wash "a minimum of three times per year."[32]

On October 24, 1977, a transit authority engineer told a reporter from the *New York Post* that the new solvent was "harmful to people who come in contact with it."[33] The engineer stated that he had stood one hundred feet downwind from the Coney Island yard train-wash machine while the graffiti solvent was in use and had "experienced a dry throat, headache, dizziness and burning eyes."[34] He continued, "any track workers required to work relatively close to the car wash machines, as well as civilians just outside TA property, are susceptible to the mist when the wind is blowing in their direction."[35] And an administrator at John Dewey High School, which is adjacent to the Coney Island yard, noted that the mist from the train washer drifted into the school's athletic yard and that "students have been forbidden to play ball there," although he added that this rule was frequently broken.[36]

MTA spokesman Louis Collins replied to charges that the new solvent was a health hazard: "I'm not saying there is no smell in the area. You are aware of it, but it is not that concentrated or obnoxious."[37] When questioned about the solvent's potential to do harm to the motorman assigned to drive the trains through the wash, Collins replied, "The spraying is a very quick thing, the motorman may be exposed only about a half-hour a day."[38] But on November 1 John deRoos ordered use of the graffiti solvent suspended for two weeks "in order to allow an industrial hygienist to study the effects of the chemical on those who are exposed to it."[39] The *New York Times* reported him as saying that "he hoped it would not prove to be harmful to humans, 'because it works.' " DeRoos had decided to halt temporarily use of the solvent after two weeks of discussions with Jack Metzger, principal of Dewey High School, who had informed him that "parents of his students had complained . . . that their children were suffering from respiratory ailments that they believed to be caused by the chemical used in the yard."[40] Metzger, also interviewed by the *Times*, stated, "At first the Transit Authority said they would keep their facility open pending their analysis, but later I persuaded them that it might be more prudent to suspend all use of the fluid until the test results were in."[41]

There was no further press coverage of the matter. According to MTA maintenance foreman Reginald Lewis, tests on the solvent were performed by the Industrial Hygienists Corporation of Lynbrook, New York, and their report stated that the chemical represented "no possible health hazard." According to Lewis use of the solvent was resumed two weeks after the initial shutdown and since that time, use of it had been expanded to six train-washing facilities around the city.

The solvent may not be harmful to humans, but it has apparently done substantial damage to some MTA equipment. In an interview at a Bronx train yard, an MTA engineer said that "the damned graffiti solvent is causing constant problems. The solvent is so powerful that it dissolves the plastic valves in the sprayer pumps. We're having new ones designed, in stainless steel, but in the meantime the valves are going out every couple of days and it takes about a half-day to replace them." When the trains are run through the water, he said, the solvent tends to leak into the cars between the rubber door guards and "after a while, if you don't mop it up right away, it just eats through the floor—through the linoleum and the concrete liner, right down to the steel shell. We've had seven cars, new ones, R-46's, in the shop getting new floors this fall because of this. That's about fifteen thousand dollars a shot. It's taking a lot of that new paint off the cars too. Amazing stuff."

Despite John deRoos's promise in 1975 that the MTA would reduce substantially its expenditures on graffiti cleaning, it appears that such costs instead rose. DeRoos stated in 1978 that the authority "is spending fifteen million dollars a year to rid cars of graffiti,"[42] a substantial increase over the estimated $7 million spent for the same purpose in 1975.[43] The figure rose even higher in 1979, when the MTA substantially increased its train-washing activities in celebration of its Diamond Jubilee Year.[44]

In May 1980 Steven Kauffman, senior executive officer of the transit authority, sent a memo to transit authority general superintendent Charles Kalkhof in which he stated, "MTA Chairman Richard Ravitch and I are looking for a way to show the public what they are getting for the recent fare increase. We need something that will provide immediate, visible results. So far the best idea appears to be: get the interior graffiti off the cars."[45]

Kalkhof responded with a $5.1 million "Graffiti and Enhancement Program," that called for the hiring of 205 car painters and 11 foremen to paint the interiors of 1,000 subway cars with epoxy paint. Although the epoxy was not as graffiti-resistant as the special polyurethane paint the transit authority normally used for interior painting, it was odorless and fast drying and would enable the authority to turn out forty freshly painted cars per day rather than their usual output of fourteen cars per week.

The plan was announced to the public on July 21. Transit authority executive director John Simpson told the *Daily News*, "We are going to repaint the interiors of the cars faster than the graffiti artists can vandalize them."[46] The newspaper responded to the announcement the following day with an editorial in which it declared that the repainting program sounded like the story of "the child who tried to empty the ocean with a bucket," and called for the authority to spend its money instead on more policemen to combat "what straphangers hate even more than graffiti: subway violence."[47]

Meanwhile, the authority's hopes for good publicity were dashed when the *Daily News* and *New York Post* revealed that tens of thousands of gallons of toxic graffiti solvents were being dumped daily by the authority into the city's waterways through unauthorized connections with the storm sewer system. The *Daily News* stated that "the waste is a combination of acid, phosphates, and xylene, a chemical that is known to cause blood damage and eye and respiratory irritation. The chemicals are used in cleaning graffiti off of subway cars at seven locations in four boroughs."[48] The transit authority responded that it was not aware that the chemicals were toxic nor that its hookups to the sewer system were illegal and promised to look into the matter further. No further statement on the matter was made.

In October the *New York Post* reported that Richard Ravitch had announced to the National Conference on Mass Transit Crime and Vandalism that "his $5 million program had flopped." A transit authority engineer explained, "The kids re-covered the cars with graffiti as fast as we could paint them. They were right to call this the Graffiti and Enhancement Program because all we did was enhance the graffiti by giving it a clean, nonresistant background."

Since that time the transit authority has limited its cleaning activities to what it calls "normal graffiti maintenance," a program that costs approximately six million dollars a year. Commenting on his earlier, more expensive efforts to completely eradicate graffiti, Ravitch said, "When I took this job I said, 'If there's one thing I'm going to do, it's get rid of the graffiti.' It's obviously not going to be one of my great successes."[50]

Graffiti squad officer Conrad Lesnewski expressed his view of the current state of the MTA's graffiti clean-up program:

Well, there are thousands and thousands of trains and they're starting to give up on them because they won't last twenty-four hours after they're painted. They had this chemical where you drive the train through and the chemical washes the graffiti paint right off without touching the paint of the train and that was working fantastic. . . . You'd see a train going through that once or twice and it would come out with all the graffiti off it, except maybe for a little bit of the real thick stuff at the bottom. And the kids lost heart. . . .

So one of the guys in these [graffiti] groups said that's no problem, so they would actually go out and they would spray an area, maybe a six-foot-square area, with a clear base epoxy first, that dries almost instantly. Then they would do their graffiti writing on top of it, then they would spray it with clear shellack when they were finished. And so you'd need a hammer and chisel to get that paint off, and that was their answer to the game. So like I say, we try to keep one jump ahead of them, but they keep one jump ahead of us, and we spend millions of dollars on research. These kids are very ingenious.

The Police

Ted Pearlman

The New York City Transit Police Department (TP) is responsible for maintaining law and order on MTA property, particularly the subways. Its force of over 3,000 officers is trained, uniformed, and equipped in a manner similar to the New York City Police Department (NYPD). The TP, however, is considered to be an independent entity, separate from the NYPD, and has its own chief and senior officers, all under the direct authority of the MTA chairman.

Beginning in 1971 the arrest of graffiti vandals became, in transit police chief Sanford Garelik's words, "a major concern of the Transit Police Department." Under the urging of Mayor Lindsay and MTA chairman William Ronan, the TP assigned more than one hundred officers to graffiti patrol duty at various transit facilities.

Chief Garelik called the arrest record achieved by this graffiti force "highly impressive." The total number of graffiti arrests rose from 351 in 1971 to 1,562 in 1972, dipped slightly to 1,408 in 1973, and then rose again to 1,652 in 1974. Of the total number of writers arrested from 1972 to 1974, more than one-third were sentenced to spend one or more days on a clean-up detail. The rest were released.

The most impressive record of arrests achieved by an individual member of the TPD was that of transit patrolman Steven Schwartz, who singlehandedly apprehended thirteen graffiti writers in the first seven months of 1972. In an interview with the *Daily News* Schwartz attributed his success to a knowledge of the behavior patterns of the writers. He "questioned the suspects at length and arrested them. But before he booked them he made . . . entries in his extensive graffiti notebook, a notebook which now contains information regarding such underground stars as Ray-B 954, Sweet Duke 161, Phase 2, Pinto 168, and Kool Kevin I."[2]

On August 28, 1972, Mayor Lindsay commended Schwartz for the initiative and dedication he showed in his pursuit of graffiti writers. At a ceremony in his office Mayor Lindsay presented Schwartz with a certificate of commendation and stated: "I want to express my personal gratitude and the thanks of all New Yorkers to this concerned and conscientious officer who obviously cares about our City. Everyone has a role to play if we are to stop vandals from thoughtlessly disfiguring buildings, buses, monuments and subways in New

York City. I hope the civic pride and spirit shown by Patrolman Schwartz will serve as an example that every New Yorker has a part to play in caring for the appearance of our city."[3]

Among those arrested by Schwartz were a number of prominent Bronx writers, including some of Bama's friends. Bama had this to say about Schwartz:

> Schwartz sprayed Sky 3. . . . He had asked . . . Sky 3 what was in this can he had 'cause one of the cans had the label peeled off, so he said "Afro Sheen." So the guy opened the top, grabbed the guy, put him in a headlock and sprayed—the guy had a big Afro—sprayed red paint all over this guy's Afro. Then told him to take his pic, pic his hair, so that it would knot up. Then he wouldn't let him touch it so that when it dried he had to cut off all his hair. That was unnecessary, that wasn't his job to do that . . .
>
> The Marquis de Schwartz. He was strange. He was a demonic little fellow. . . . He had this thing about capturing all the big known graffiti writers. His thing was so strong because people were backing him. He was getting backing by the big cheeses in the police department, in the transit department. He was being backed by the mayor and a lot of other city agencies were praising this man for his work cleaning these insane beasts off the streets. And because that was going down, it gave him the freedom to treat us the way he wanted. And if he had a bad day, and didn't get no poo or something like that, he took it out on us, especially people like El Marko who he knew. And if he seen him on the train going to work, he would get harassed. He'd walk up to El Marko and say, "Let me see what you got in your pocket." "I ain't got nothing." "Let me see what you got in your pocket! Get off the fucking train. Now!" You don't need no shit like that.

El Marko's difficulties with Schwartz continued until his good friend Lionel stepped in and resolved the matter on his behalf. Bama explained:

> El Marko had gotten busted. He was on the platform at 180th Street looking pitiful. Schwartz had him by the arm. We were in the front of the train and we saw them as

we pulled in. Lionel was with us, so what does he do? He runs back through the train to where Schwartz and El Marko are standing and gets there before the doors opened, crouched low so they can't see him. When the doors opened Lionel just stood up, said, "Hello Patrolman Schwartz," and hit him, pow, right in the face. It was so beautiful. We were looking out the doors up front and all we saw was Schwartz and El Marko standing there and Lionel's fist coming out the door while the other hand is pulling El Marko in. Schwartz went down and then the doors closed and we were gone.

In January 1973 Schwartz was assigned by the TPD to "set up an education program instructing youngsters and community groups of the intensity of the graffiti problem."[4] Questioned by a *Daily News* reporter as to the progress of the fight against graffiti, Schwartz replied that "the graffiti problem is a major one, but not unsolvable . . . the increasing number of arrests, the toughened stand of the courts and the interest of the Mayor have the graffiti problem on the wane."

The Graffiti Squad

After 1974 the number of graffiti arrests by the transit police declined rapidly. In 1975 1,202 writers were arrested, in 1976, 799, and in 1977, 348. The reasons for this decrease in apprehensions have been explained by transit police public information officer Edward Silverfarb:

> The transit police was faced with a manpower reduction. There were layoffs because of the city budget crisis . . . There was overall a 19% reduction in the transit police force, as a result of attrition and layoffs and a job freeze. So we were forced to reconsider our priorities and reevaluate what we were doing with our manpower. We felt we couldn't devote quite so much manpower to the graffiti problem as a result of this reduction in force. We also found that though we may make many arrests, we felt the courts, the criminal justice system wasn't really giving it the kind of attention the problem required to be effective. And so that was another reason for easing up on the arrests.

Although the TP was forced to divert officers from graffiti patrols to other more pressing duties, graffiti was still considered to be a major concern, and a new appoach to the problem was sought that would be more efficient and less costly in personnel than the previous large-scale mass arrest formula. Their solution was to establish a special unit consisting of officers assigned to seek out and apprehend major writers. A graffiti squad consisting of ten plainclothes officers under the command of Detective Sergeant Morris Bitchachi was formed in 1975. Police officers Michael Bianco and Theodore Rotun outlined the objectives and tactics of the squad:

Bianco:

We're out there on patrol in plainclothes, looking for where these kids are writing, when they're writing, what they're writing. They had a graffiti squad before but it wasn't doing as much as we were; they were just in the yards for the graffiti problem. But we're out there more, sometimes talking with the kids, finding out more about graffiti, why they're writing and all that stuff.

Rotun:

I would say we're more an intelligence type of operation; we find out the methods, how they operate. We infiltrate. It's a regular big operation. . . . We know where they live, how they live, what schools they go to, where they work; we keep files. We assist various other police departments in naming the graffiti artists. We have the biggest graffiti file, I guess, in the world.

Bianco:

Also now our policy is, let's just say that we're really not after the small-fry. We're gonna be after the big-fry.

They gathered information about the writers by a variety of means. Much of it was derived from the questioning of apprehended writers. Some was provided by informers who "dropped dimes" on fellow writers for personal reasons. One of the most important means of acquiring information about graffiti was informal conversation and socializing between officers and writers. Officer Bianco explained, "Some of them, when they're at the writers' corners, we sit down and we talk with them, and you know, they talk to you. . . . [we] find out what's going on. . . . I have this 'black book' over here, where the kids, when they sit at the corner, they pass it around, they get each kid's autograph. You know, I myself have one, where when I see these kids, I have them write in my book."

Sergeant Bitchachi claimed the squad's graffiti file contained over 3,000 photographs of various writers' styles, which, he stated, "are just like fingerprints. We can identify a writer's work, even if he has changed his name, by examining it and comparing it to the samples in the files." The file also contained the names, both given and writing, home addresses, schools, arrest records, and other pertinent information on over 1,500 writers. Graffiti squad officers made a point of learning not only the writer's graffiti names but their real names as well, which Conrad Lesnewski said is useful in making apprehensions: "We'll see a kid writing and we'll yell, 'Hey, Joey Smith, don't run! We know you. We'll get you at home anyway.' That usually stops them."[5]

If a writer ran away, graffiti squad officers sometimes chased him. But if the officers knew the writer's home address, they would instead let the culprit escape and then go to his home and arrest him there. Officer Kevin Hickey has explained that some writers could be captured in this manner even in cases where their specific addresses were not known: "You might not know where a kid lives but if you go to his area, it's like following bloodstains. You follow walls where their names are written, and they'll lead you right up to the kid's apartment. Often the kid's graffiti name will be on the inside hallway and on the door of the apartment itself."

Many graffiti squad officers looked upon time spent getting to know the writers as one of their most important and interesting pursuits. They generally typified their other activities as routine police work." On a typical day on the graffiti squad, according to Lesnewski;

> If you don't have any court appearances or follow-up investigations, you usually come in and read the crime reports, see if there were any complaints during the nighttime, try to find out what areas are being hit, go out and make contacts with certain juveniles. You could sit on a hunch and see if it will be raided by graffiti kids. We might ride the trains for a couple of hours and go around to

the hot places, the places being hit the most. If we make a hit, we might get two or three kids and then spend the rest of the day on the arrest process. It's very time-consuming. For juveniles, there are approximately ten forms that have to be filled out, and we have to try to locate the parents. We'll ride around in the back car of a train and if we see kids hanging out in the station and we recognize one or two of them as graffiti kids, we'll get off at the next station and take a bus back to the station and we'll stay in a corner and watch what they're going to do. Maybe they're there to meet somebody, maybe they're there to smoke pot.

"Just because we're in the graffiti unit," Hickey continues, "that doesn't preclude us from doing other police work. There have been many times when we've been riding on trains and we've seen something else go down and we'll take police action. We've picked up bagsnatchers and armed robbers, whatever the case may be."

Following their own hunches or tips provided by informers, graffiti squad officers occasionally staked out a yard or lay-up at which they expected graffiti writing to take place. Hickey and Lesnewski described the process in detail:

Lesnewski:

We'll cover a place alone or get two guys from the graffiti squad sent up from Brooklyn. We'll tell them we might have a party here tonight.

Hickey:

We generally shy away from the uniformed policemen and anticrime officers because they don't have the expertise to handle this. Graffiti might sound trivial but there is a fair amount of danger involved with these trains, and if you have a person who is not knowledgeable about the track area they could get seriously hurt. That's one reason. Another reason is that they can just get in your way. You don't want to trip over other officers.

Lesnewski:

When kids come into a yard, say in Baychester, they might have a party of ten to fifteen kids. We might be sitting there, my partner and I, if we have a rumor or a hunch. There might be two or three guys, cops, with fifteen kids coming in. One of us will be in the front of the train sitting on the floor with the door just cracked, keeping a lookout. A patrolman might be in the middle of the train, looking at a hole in the fence, and the other guy will be in the back of the train. The kids will always send one kid ahead as a lookout while the rest are back in the woods or all strung out. They'll send up one youth, he's the scout, he'll come up very cautiously looking both ways, he'll go up and walk toward the train very cautiously, and he'll look under the train, and in the back and along the sides of the train. He'll go to the other side of the train to four or six other trains and check them out. He'll climb on the top of one train and look out on the roof, come back, wait a couple of minutes, and then he'll go back to the bushes, walk back to the train and look again, and then the others will approach the train cautiously . . . in small groups, two or three at a time. We'll let them set up, and then we'll jump down out of the train, but if they see anything suspicious, like someone smoking a cigarette, they'll take off at ninety miles an hour.

Hickey:

When you jump down on them, the kids scatter like rats. Some will go under the trains, some will climb up on top of the trains and run the whole length of the train from the top. Others will run along the rails or jump over the fences.

Lesnewski:

You're holding on to a fifteen-year-old kid, the kid may be 140, 150 pounds and he's scrambling to get loose, and you're scrambling to get a hold on him and you can't just cuff him to the train 'cause of the third rail there and you have to worry about his safety. So you have to take him down out of the yard and cuff him to a fence so you can go back and regroup and check up on your partner to make sure your partner's not hurt. While this is going on, nobody's stopping the trains and they're still going by. So the safety factor is a very big thing. The kids are crawling under the trains and the safety factor doesn't mean anything to them, but he's not going to take me with him or viceversa.

The graffiti squad considered its work to be important for a number of reasons. Primary among these was the fact that there is a city law against graffiti writing and that, as a legally defined crime, the police are obligated to do everything in their power to combat it. A second reason, and the one most frequently cited, was that train yards and lay-ups are dangerous places and that writers who enter them expose themselves to serious harm. The graffiti squad thus saw as one of its most important missions the need to keep writers out of harm's way. Police officers Bianco and Rotun described the dangers of the yards and lay-ups:

Rotun:

When they go into a lay-up, sometimes the lay-up [the train] is moved. Or say, a train is on a northbound track; that doesn't mean the train can't be coming down the track southbound. . . . You could slip, you could get your foot caught in a switching track. You never know when they're going to try out the switches. They don't realize the danger. It's like someone of fifteen or fourteen, he doesn't really in his mind realize the dangers involved.

Bianco:

There's the danger of being electrocuted too. From the power from the third rail, 'cause there's a third rail and then there's what's called a running board, the wood board that's over it. They stand on that to paint the trains.

Rotun:

And sometimes that board can give, it gets rotted away. . . . And say, like when it's wet, and you're running around outdoors and you're jumping from track to track, the electricity leaks. There's a certain amount of leakage, and if you get caught by that, it could knock you for a loop. See, I never knew that until one day we found out the hard way. . . wetness is a conductor of electricity. You see, they don't realize that . . . that's one of the things they don't realize.

A third reason for antigraffiti activity on the part of the police was provided by transit police chief Garelik who in 1976 ordered a survey taken of the police records of 413 people who had been arrested for graffiti writing as fifteen year olds in

1974. Of those surveyed, 73 (17.6 percent) were found to have been later arrested for felonies and 41 (9.9 percent) had been arrested for misdemeanors. This survey was not publicized. A second survey, taken in 1977, found that of 748 writers arrested in 1975, 213 (28.78 percent) had gone on to commit felonies and 80 (10.81 percent) had gone on to misdemeanors. Garelik called a news conference and informed the press that the 1977 survey "destroys the romantic myth that graffiti writing is a harmless act."[6] He was further quoted as saying that "it is predictable that a young graffiti writer will become a criminal." In a later interview Garelik stated that the 1977 survey proved that "graffiti writing is a school for crime." He continued, "Graffiti has been shown statistically to lead directly to harder crimes . . . to ignore this fact is to do a serious injustice to the public."

The squad continued to combat graffiti until 1979 when it was disbanded. No reasons for the dissolution of the squad have been officially given. Kevin Hickey believes they "were needed in other areas. There's been a cutback in personnel. . . . Ski, Rotun and I were absorbed into the Juvenile Crime Prevention Unit; some went to the regular anticrime division. Sergeant Bitchachi went back to the detective division. Bianco and a couple of the other guys went back in uniform, out on patrol at the stations. That's like purgatory after plainclothes."

Hickey and Ski

Graffiti squad officers Kevin Hickey and Conrad Lesnewski (known to just about everyone as "Ski") were, to the writers in the Bronx, the two most famous policemen in New York City. Dea-2 said of them, "They're like super-cops, like Starsky and Hutch [popular television detectives]. . . . They'll swing down onto writers from the elevated tracks to catch them, or grab them right in the yards. . . . They know all sorts of stuff about us, they're like writers themselves." "All the graffiti writers know them," said Mitch. "All of them. They've got fame. They've been in the newspaper before. Some people write 'For Hickey and Ski' on the pieces or sometimes they'll write, 'Hickey and Ski suck.' " Rat continued, "and if Hickey and Ski see it they go to the corners and find out who it was. And usually they find who did it but they don't do nothing about it. I think they like it."

Working out of a base of operations in the TPD's district 11 headquarters on the lower level of the Yankee Stadium (161st Street) subway station in the Bronx, Hickey and Ski began their careers as graffiti squad officers in mid-1975. The two officers quickly established a daily routine of going on graffiti patrols—traveling throughout the borough, meeting, conversing with, and, when appropriate, arresting many writers.

Within a short time Hickey and Ski noticed that the writers they encountered (even those whom they had not previously met) seemed to admire them, even to the extent of considering it, in Hickey's words, "a compliment to be arrested by Hickey and Ski." As their arrest rate and circle of writing acquaintances grew, Hickey and Ski discovered that most of the Bronx writers considered them to be famous cops and worthy opponents.

Hickey and Ski have attributed their fame among the writers to the personal relationships that they established with them:

Hickey:

> With these kids, at least the kids we run across in the Bronx, you might arrest them on a Thursday, but that doesn't mean that if we see them on Friday, we're automatically their enemy. We try to maintain a rapport with them, that the police are not the bad guys. Just because I've arrested you doesn't mean I'm your enemy for the rest of your life. We sit down and rap with them, talk over their problems, ask them how it went in court, and how their family took it. We'll buy them a soda, a piece of cake, whatever. Also by talking with them, we gather valuable information on how they think and what might be the next time they're going to do a job. So if you make them your enemy and get them to where you can't talk with them, you'll lose a very valuable avenue of information. But if you stay their friends, you can pump them for more information, unbeknownst to them.

Lesnewski:

> We try to build up their confidence in us. And our confidence in them, that they are somebody. We also tell them,

hey just because you were locked up by us last night doesn't mean that you've got to tell everybody that. We're not goin' to tell anybody 'cause it's your personal business. If you want to brag that you were locked up, go ahead and do it; we don't. After all, we do our job and they do theirs and they seem to understand this.

Through hours of conversation with writers, Hickey and Ski acquired an extensive knowledge of their lore, life-styles, and habits, information they applied to their police work. In one early case, for example, Hickey and Ski took advantage of one group of writers' desire for instant fame in setting a trap for them. Hickey explained:

This was an incident when the squad was first started and the kids didn't know any of the cops that were working graffiti. So one kid had been arrested in Queens and we were taking some pictures of what he had written to be used in court. While we were taking the pictures, some kids were over by the fence and they said, "Hey what are you doing, taking pictures of the trains? Are you newspaper men?" . . . We said, "Yeah, we're with the newspapers. We're doing a story on graffiti." So the kids said, "We do graffiti. You want to see us paint?" So we said, "No, no, we're not interested." . . . They said, "Well, we're going to be here on Saturday, painting. Why don't you come by and take some pictures?" "Since you already have this plan, maybe we will stop by on Saturday morning, and if you're here we'll take your picture." So sure enough, on Saturday morning the kids were there painting. We took some pictures from the right and some pictures from the left and some pictures from behind and when they were finished, we said, "Oh by the way, you're under arrest. We're police officers." And they said, "Hey you can't do that. You're not playing fair." But we hadn't induced them to do it, and now we just had firsthand evidence.

The arrest record of the two officers eventually came to be the most impressive of any of the squad members. The writers were well aware of this fact, and many of them attributed Hickey and Ski's high apprehension rate to the help they received from a vast network of paid informers. Hickey and Ski were questioned about their use of informers in a recent interview:

Interviewer:

Do you ever get tips?

Lesnewski:

It depends on the kid's reliability, his credibility.

Hickey:

We have found out from prior experience that a lot of times they will call stating that one place is going to be hit, so when we go and cover that area, they hit someplace else. It's a subterfuge.

Interviewer:

Why would a kid give you a real tip?

Hickey:

You might have a kid, a small kid or a kid who's starting out, who has been roughed up by another graffiti artist or who has done work and has been written over by other graffiti artists and they want to get even. There are two ways of getting even: they can either fight them personally and have a knockdown-dragout fight. But if the kid isn't big enough to take care of himself, he might drop a dime on the kid and get him arrested.

Lesnewski:

One more thing is that when you get a tip, you can't give the kid anything monetary or any breaks or favors. If the kid who gave you a tip is caught in the yards the next day, he's arrested like anybody else. We have a lot of kids who get caught by uniformed officers doing something minor and say, "I know Ski and Hickey," like they're trying to say they work for us, which is not true. There are no special provisions here for informers—no money, no nothing. It's not like the detective division.

Interviewer:

Would you like to have paid information?

Lesnewski:

I guess it would probably make the work easier, but I don't think it's a good idea 'cause you'd have kids setting up other kids. If you gave a kid five dollars for informing, he'd go out and get younger kids and give them some paint and set them up. He'd become like a bounty hunter.

Hickey:

You also have to be very careful of entrapment—when you induce or encourage somebody else to commit a crime. After all, we want to stop graffiti, not induce kids to do it just so we can apprehend them. After all, it's no joke to arrest somebody; it's a traumatic experience.

Hickey and Ski also took advantage of their powers of observation in finding and capturing writers. One time a graffiti patrol ended in a spectacular chase:

Hickey:

We were on the northbound Woodlawn train and we passed by the station. We were in the last car when we noticed there were a group of kids on the platform, and when the train doors opened, the kids didn't get on. So we stayed there and on the next station, we got off. So we walked back from the next station and Ski stayed down in the street and I went up to the station and I said, "I'll chase them from where they are, and they'll probably shimmy down the el pillar and you can catch them at the bottom." So as I get toward them, sure enough, they go down the el pole, so I yell out to "Connie, they're coming down." These kids are like monkeys. So a couple of these kids are halfway down the pillar, getting filthy dirty but they look down and see Connie there and just as fast as they were going down, they start going back up. In the meantime, I was hurrying down to give him a hand in the street. They climbed back up into the station and Connie shouts, "They're coming back up." So I start to chase them and they jump over the railing just as a train is coming in. As the kid jumped, the train couldn't have missed his leg by more than two inches. I was thinking to myself, "Oh my God, this kid is dead." But him and this other kid, they get on the catwalk and they start running.

Lesnewski:

I jumped in the car and drove down to the next station to get them, but they didn't do that. They went halfway down, between both stations, and then they shimmied down the pole and they got away.

Hickey:

These are two of the kids that beat us out. Some of the few that got away.

Lesnewski:

They'll do anything to get away. They'll climb down between the cars, or down the pillars. Sometimes they'll lift up the seats on the trains and hide under the seats. They have something about being caught, and they'll take incredible chances.

Hickey:

If this had been a regular group, we wouldn't have chased them. We would have just called out to them and they would have known it was us, and they would have known that running away would be futile 'cause we know their real names and addresses. But these were two new guys and they didn't know us.

Hickey's and Ski's pursuit of writers was hazardous not only for the writers but for the two officers themselves. Even a quiet stake-out had dangers, as Hickey has explained:

I don't recall if we got a tip on it or if it was a hot spot. You know there are some spots where the kids will go every weekend, come hell or hot water. And there were three of us, the sergeant and us two playing this area. And we were inside the train waiting for the kids to come in. So when the scout comes in, we stayed down low and kept as quiet as possible. In the meantime, another group started coming in from the other side and they started painting on the other side of the train. The scout didn't see them, didn't see anything so he brought the rest of his group in. So we had five kids on one side of the train painting and ten kids on the other side of the train painting. And we're inside this train and the fumes, they're toxic, and we were getting dizzy. It's like sniffing glue. We didn't know which way to turn. If we opened one side, the kids would run away from the other side. So we finally worked out a plan where we opened both doors at once and we grabbed one kid from one group and two kids from the other group. And with the information supplied by these kids, we were able to lock up all fifteen of them. But the fumes were so bad that we were forced to make a move, whether we wanted to or not, just to get some fresh air.

The actions of writers did not represent the only threat to the safety of graffiti squad officers. There were other dangers as well:

Hickey:

There are some comical dangers involved in the police work. In the beginning when we went to a train yard, we've had instances where . . . plainclothes graffiti cops would be walking in the yard and some of them would take a shortcut and would walk through these train washers. So the transit personnel would see strangers in the yard and they're very paranoid and they'd think they were beakies or shooflies [MTA inspectors] out after them. So we had one cop, he walked through this, and they turned on the washer on him, he got soaked and he got a little mad. So now we know that before we go into these yards, we have to identify ourselves to these people, to let them know we're not out checking up on them on their job. We've had instances in big yards where we'd be walking through and we've identified ourselves to the foremen; before word had spread, we'd see other people, and they'd see us and not knowing who we were, they would run, literally just run away as if they were kids themselves, thinking we were out to spy on them.

Lesnewski:

They'll start blowing the whistles on the trains to signal each other, to let each other know there are plainclothes men in the yard.

Hickey:

I had an incident once. My partner was on vacation, and I was up on the Concourse yards and it's a wooded area off to the side. And I was more or less in the wooded area waiting for the kids to come down, and some of these transit personnel saw me and I don't know if they thought I was a bum or a beakie or one of their bosses, but before I knew it there were rocks being thrown at me. I felt like David and Goliath; I was being stoned to death.

In 1979 when the graffiti squad was disbanded, Hickey and Ski were reassigned to the Juvenile Crime Prevention Unit, which seeks to divert young people from criminal activities through, Kevin Hickey said, "counseling and aid from the unit's staff and a variety of social service agencies." The purpose of the unit is to free the juvenile courts from the responsibility of having to process young people who are charged with minor crimes by diverting them to a variety of counseling and educational programs.

Both Hickey and Ski found their new work challenging but missed their days on the graffiti squad. Both preferred their earlier investigative work to the sort of "desk jockeying" to which they were assigned. They also, as Kevin Hickey lamented, "miss the writers." Lesnewski found his work on the graffiti squad "very interesting and very challenging. I'd like to help these kids. I do think they need help. And the graffiti unit is trying to help them, but the graffiti unit is on a blank road. The courts and the social system here is nothing, it's a one-way street, lock them up, put them in court and let them out. Something should be done." Hickey concurred: "The graffiti unit has afforded us a unique opportunity to spend time with these kids, not just lock them up and put them away but really try to relate to these kids, to spend the time to try and figure out what makes them kick, see what problems they have and hopefully help them to resolve some of these problems, help them out, find them jobs. This is more diversified than just police work, there is also some social work in it."

In fall 1980 the TP formed a new, five-man graffiti squad under the direction of Sergeant Frank Williams. Hickey and Ski were not invited to join the unit and instead were assigned, after the demise of the Juvenile Crime Prevention Unit in December 1980, to plainclothes duty at TP district twelve in the Bronx. Although they spend very little time on antigraffiti efforts, they do pass along information from their informants and give advice to members of the new graffiti unit.

Ted Pearlman

A Final Note

During the period of time covered by this book, New York City suffered from financial troubles that drove it to the verge of bankruptcy and necessitated severe cutbacks in municipal spending. It seems logical to ask why, in times of fiscal crisis, the city found it necessary to wage an expensive and ineffective war against subway graffiti. Mayor Koch justified his anti-graffiti expenditures by declaring that the elimination of graffiti would have a "positive psychological impact"[1] on subway riders. More detailed speculations on the psychological impact of subway graffiti were made by Harvard University sociologist Nathan Glazer, who wrote,

> I have not interviewed the subway riders; but I am one myself, and while I do not find myself consciously making the connection between the graffiti-makers and the criminals who occasionally rob, rape, and assault passengers, the sense that all are part of one world of uncontrollable predators seems inescapable. Even if the graffitists are the least dangerous of these, their ever-present markings serve to persuade the passenger that, indeed, the subway is a dangerous place . . . .
>
> The issue of controlling graffiti is not only one of protecting public property . . . but also one of reducing the ever-present sense of fear, of making the subway appear a less dangerous and unpleasant place to the possible user.[2]

MTA Chairman Richard Ravitch, agreeing with Glazer's view, said, "I fully understand that graffiti is not in the same category as murder or robbery. However, it is a symbol that we have lost control. If we are to regain control of our system, we must have the assistance of the media in portraying graffiti for what it is — a wanton act of vandalism that should be punishable by incarceration."[3]

Daze responded to Ravitch's statement, saying, "The public doesn't waste its time worrying about graffiti, they've got other things to worry about. The public's got to understand that if the MTA could get rid of graffiti it wouldn't make the subways any safer, or make them smell any better, or clean up the garbage, or get rid of the noise or make the muggers and bums go away. If the MTA really understood graffiti, they'd know that it's one of the best, things the subways have going for them. If the city would back us up and treat us as artists instead of vandals, we could contribute a lot to the beauty of New York."

Lee, expanding on this point, said:

If they didn't buff the trains, then every car would have a whole-car and the people would like that. It would be like Disneyworld on tracks, and be one of the serious things to see in New York. People would come from all over just to look at it. When the city designed the subway system they made some bad choices on colors. The trains look really depressing painted silver-gray and blue. An effort should have been made to make them look good. Like the whole train I painted, I think a lot of people thought it was a test train to try out a new design and it made a lot of people think. If the subways were painted nice, it would make a lot of people very happy. Like you walk out of your house and you look at nice pieces and it eases your mind. The colors are alive so you feel alive with them. We've got to keep on painting the trains no matter what.

In summer 1981 Zephyr, Ali, and a number of other writers asked the MTA to allow them to decorate one subway train, under Transit Authority supervision, and measure public response to it with an eye toward painting the rest of the trains if the public approved. Richard Ravitch later commented on their proposal, saying, "I know what the public response to their idea would be; they'd hate it. I talk to a lot of citizens groups and I'm always asked about graffiti — as desecration. The subways in general are a mess, and the public sees graffiti as a form of deterioration like garbage, noise, dirt, and broken doors. I have an obligation to respect the rights of the public and they all hate graffiti."

Notes

Chapter 2

1. Hugo Martinez, "A Brief Background of Graffiti," in *United Graffiti Artists 1975.*

Chapter 4

1. "Divine Graffiti," *New York Post,* November 29, 1978, p. 31.

2. Hugo Martinez. "A Brief Background of Graffiti," in *United Graffiti Artists 1975.*

Chapter 5

1. Donald Jackson, "Youth Gangs' Violence Found Rising in Three Cities," *New York Times,* April 16, 1972, p. 58.

2. James Haskins, *Street Gangs* (New York: Hastings House, 1974), p. 139.

3. Ibid, p. 7.

Chapter 6

1. Hugo Martinez, "A Brief Background of Graffiti," in *United Graffiti Artists 1975* catalog.

2. Ibid.

3. Ibid.

4. Ibid.

5. Ibid.

6. Roger Ricklefs, "Co-Co 144's Underground Art School," *Wall Street Journal,* April 26, 1973, p. 40.

7. James Ryan, "The Great Graffiti Plague, " *New York Daily News,* May 6, 1973, p. 33.

8. Peter Schjeldahl, "Graffiti Goes Legit—But the 'Show-Off' Ebullience Remains," *New York Times,* September 16, 1973, p. 27.

9. S. K. Overbeck, "Underground Artists," *Newsweek,* October 1, 1973, p. 70.

10. Martinez, "A Brief Background."

11. Sandy Satterwhite, "For Them Graffiti Is No Longer an Underground Movement," *New York Post,* December 24, 1974.

Chapter 7

1. Quoted in David Freeman, "Slop Art," *New York Times Magazine,* November 26, 1972, p. 16.

2. "'Taki 183' Spawns Pen Pals," *New York Times,* July 21, 1971, p. 37.

3. Ibid.

4. "Garelik Calls for War on Graffiti," *New York Times,* May 21, 1972, p. 66.

5. "Nuisance in Technicolor," *New York Times*, May 26, 1972, p. 34.

6. "Fines and Jail for Graffiti Will Be Asked by Lindsay," *New York Times*, June 26, 1972, p. 66.

7. "Lindsay Assails Graffiti Vandals," *New York Times*, August 25, 1972, p. 30.

8. Edward Ranzal, "Officials Testify in Favor of Mayor's Graffiti Bill," *New York Times*, September 1, 1972, p. 25.

9. Edward Ranzal, "Ronan Backs Lindsay Antigraffiti Plan," *New York Times*, August 29, 1972, p. 66.

10. Ibid.

11. "Stiff Antigraffiti Measure Passes Council Committee," *New York Times*, September 15, 1972, p. 41.

12. New York Administrative Code, Section 435-13.2 (1972).

13. "Stiff Administrative Measure Passes Council Committee," *New York Times*, September 15, 1972, p. 41.

14. "Scratch the Graffiti," *New York Times*, September 16, 1972, p. 28.

15. "Lindsay Forms 'Graffiti Task Force,'" *New York Times*, October 5, 1972, p. 51.

16. Office of Mayor John V. Lindsay, press release, October 4, 1972.

17. "Antigraffiti Bill One of Four Gaining Council Approval," *New York Times*, October 11, 1972, p. 47.

18. "Lindsay Signs Graffiti Bill," *New York Times*, October 28, 1972, p. 15.

19. "New Chemical May Curb Graffiti," *New York Times*, April 22, 1972, p. 35.

20. Office of Mayor John V. Lindsay, press release, July 31, 1972.

21. "Antigraffiti 'Bucket Brigade' Planned," *New York Times*, November 13, 1972, p. 41.

22. "Boy Scouts Scrub Graffiti off Walls of Subway Cars," *New York Times*, February 25, 1973, p. 35.

23. E. H. Sachs, Jr., letter, *New York Times*, December 24, 1972, Sec. 8, p. 2.

24. M. W. Covington, letter, *New York Times*, December 26, 1972, p. 32.

25. R. H. Robinson, letter, *New York Times*, June 5, 1972, p. 32.

26. P. R. Patterson, letter, *New York Times*, December 14, 1972, p. 46.

27. *New York Times*, January 14, 1973, p. 14.

28. "Fight against Subway Graffiti Progresses from Frying Pan to Fire," *New York Times*, January 26, 1973, p. 39.

29. Bureau of the Budget of the City of New York, *Work Plan—Graffiti Prevention Project* (February 26, 1973), p. 2.

30. Ibid., p. 3.

31. Ibid., p. 2.

32. Richard Goldstein, "This Thing Has Gotten Completely Out of Hand," *New York Magazine*, March 26, 1973, pp. 35–39.

33. "The Graffiti 'Hit' Parade," *New York Magazine*, March 26, 1973, pp. 40–43.

34. Murray Schumach, "At $10 Million, City Calls It a Losing Graffiti Fight," *New York Times*, March 28, 1973, p. 46.

35. James Ryan, "The Great Graffiti Plague," *New York Daily News Sunday Magazine*, May 6, 1973, p. 33.

36. James Ryan, "The Mayor Charges MTA Is Soft on Graffiti," *New York Daily News*, July 1, 1973, p. 2.

37. Alfred E. Clark, "Persistent Graffiti Anger Lindsay on Subway Tour," *New York Times*, July 1, 1979, p. 47.

38. Ibid.

39. Norman Mailer, *The Faith of Graffiti* (New York: Praeger/Alskog Publishers, 1974).

40. Ibid.

41. Owen Moritz, "The New Subway," *New York Daily News*, December 5, 1978, p. 37.

42. George Jochnowitz, "Thousands of Child-hours Wasted on Ugly Daubings," *New York Post*, October 20, 1978, p. 43.

43. Ari L. Goldman, "Dogs to Patrol Subway Yards," *New York Times*, September 15, 1981, p. 1.

44. Ibid.

45. Ari L. Goldman, "City to Use Pits of Barbed Wire in Graffiti War," *New York Times*, December 15, 1981, p. B-1.

Chapter 8

1. James Ryan, "The Great Graffiti Plague," *New York Daily News Sunday Magazine*, May 6, 1973, p. 33.

2. Murray Schumach, "At $10 Million, City Calls It a Losing Graffiti Fight," *New York Times*, March 28, 1973, p. 46.

3. "'Taki 183' Spawns Pen Pals," *New York Times*, July 21, 1971, p. 37.

4. Edward Ranzal, "Ronan Backs Lindsay Antigraffiti Plan, Including Clean-up Duty," *New York Times*, August 29, 1972, p. 66.

5. Ryan, "Great Graffiti Plague," p. 33.

6. Ibid.

7. Robert Tomasson, "Graffiti Clean-ups a 'Lark' for the Young," *New York Times*, April 21, 1974, p. 23.

8. Lewis Grossberger, "Frank Berry Takes It Personally and He Resents the Graffiti," *New York Post*, February 15, 1974, p. 3.

9. Edward C. Burks, "MTA to Use Dogs in Its Battle on Graffiti," *New York Times*, July 30, 1974, p. 35.

10. Ibid.

11. Ibid.

12. "Going to the Dogs," *New York Times*, August 4, 1974, p. 22.

13. Frank Mazza, "Question Plan to Use Dogs to Fight Graffiti," *New York Daily News*, July 31, 1978, p. 12.

14. Tomasson, "Graffiti Clean-ups," p. 23.

15. Ibid.

16. "A Trial Run for Canines vs. Graffiti," *New York Post*, August 6, 1974, p. 7.

17. Ibid.

18. Ibid.

19. Daniel Driscoll, "The Trouble with Graffiti, It's a Catching Disease," *New York Daily News*, August 18, 1974, p. 3.

20. "Dogs and Graffiti," *New York Times*, November 24, 1974, p. 37.

21. Edward Hudson, "Yunich Says the Transit Payroll Is Down and Will Fall Further," *New York Times*, March 19, 1975, p. 28.

22. Ibid.

23. "Subway Graffiti Campaign Given Lower Priority," *New York Times*, August 7, 1975, p. 25.

24. Ibid.

25. Michael Hechtman, "New TA Paint: Graffiti Comes Off in the Wash," *New York Post*, May 11, 1976, p. 4.

26. Ibid.

27. Gus Dallas, "A Solution for Graffiti," *New York Daily News*, October, 10, 1977, p. 9.

28. Hechtman, "New TA Paint," p. 4.

29. Frank Mazza, "Future for City Graffiti Artists," *New York Daily News*, May 28, 1976, p. 6.

30. Ibid.

31. "Subway Graffiti," *New York Times*, March 20, 1977, p. 45.

32. Ibid.

33. Patrick W. Sullivan, "Anti-Graffiti Chemical Called Health Hazard," *New York Post*, October 24, 1977, p. 2.

34. Ibid.

35. Ibid.

36. Ibid.

37. Ibid.

38. Ibid.

39. "Fume Fear Halts Graffiti Work," *New York Times*, November 1, 1977, p. 27.

40. Ibid.

41. Ibid.

42. Owen Moritz and Richard Edmonds, "The New Subway Car: Fast, Quiet and Cool," *New York Times*, December 5, 1978.

43. "Subway Graffiti Campaign Given Lower Priority," *New York Times*, August 7, 1979, p. 25.

44. Moritz and Edmonds, "New Subway Car."

45. Richard Edmonds, "$5M Paint Plan Seeks to Halt Subway Graffitists in Their Tracks," *New York Daily News*, July 21, 1980, p. 2.

46. Ibid.

47. "First Things First," *New York Daily News*, July 22, 1980, p. 30.

48. Richard Edmonds, "TA Dumping Toxic Waste into City Waters," *New York Daily News*, July 17, 1980, p. 2.

49. Jeff Wells, "TA Cheers Judge for Attacking Graffiti," *New York Post*, October 25, 1980, p. 3.

50. "Who Can Do What About the Subways in New York," *New York Times*, December 13, 1981, p. 20.

Chapter 9

1. Robert Tomasson, "Graffiti Cleanups a 'Lark' for the Young," *New York Times*, April 21, 1974, p. 23.

2. Donald Singleton, "This Grime-Buster Is a 1-Man Graffiti Squad," *New York Daily News*, August 28, 1972, p. 5.

3. Office of Mayor John V. Lindsay, press release, August 28, 1972.

4. James Ryan, "Handwriting on the Wall for Graffiti? Yes, Say Police," *New York Daily News*, January 14, 1973, p. 4.

5. Gus Dallas, "Critic-Cops Go Underground to Catch a Running Art Show," *New York Daily News*, November 20, 1977, p. 10.

6. Gus Dallas, "Graffiti Writers Have Other Blots," *New York Daily News*, November 24, 1977, p. 4.

A Final Note

1. Nathan Glazer, "On Subway Graffiti In New York," *The Public Interest*, Winter 1979.

2. Richard Ravitch, "Graffiti By Any Name Is Vandalism," *New York Daily News*, November 6, 1980, p. 20.

References

Articles (in chronological order)

"'Taki 183' Spawns Pen Pals." *New York Times*, July 21, 1971.

Janson, Donald. "Spray Paint Adds to Graffiti Damage." *New York Times*, July 25, 1971.

Prial, Frank J. "Subway Graffiti Here Called Epidemic." *New York Times*, February 11, 1972.

"An Identity Thing." *Time*, March 13, 1972.

"They're Easier to Ignore Than the Authors Realize." *New York Daily News*, April 26, 1972.

"Up Against the Wall." *Newsweek*, May 8, 1972.

"Nuisance in Technicolor." *New York Times*, May 21, 1972.

"Garelick Calls for War on Graffiti." *New York Times*, May 21, 1972.

Perlmutter, Emanuel. "Fines and Jail for Graffiti Will Be Asked by Lindsay." *New York Times*, June 26, 1972.

Gelman, David. "The Children of Taki." *Newsday*, June 26, 1972.

Douris, George. "Councilmen Praise Plan to Punish Graffiti Scrawlers." *Newsday*, June 26, 1972.

"Action on Dog Litter and Graffiti Put Off for Months by Council." *New York Times*, July 6, 1972.

"Lindsay Assails Graffiti Vandals." *New York Times*, August 25, 1972.

Singleton, Donald. "This Grime-Buster Is a 1-Man Graffiti Squad." *New York Daily News*, August 28, 1972.

Shirey, David L. "Semi-Retired Graffiti Scrawlers Paint Mural at CCNY 133." *New York Times*, December 8, 1972.

Horsley, Carter B. "Washington Heights Fights Graffiti." *New York Times*, December 17, 1972.

Heller, Ernest S. "Ganging Up against Graffiti." Letter to the Editor. *New York Times*, December 24, 1972.

"St. Pat's Graffiti Suspect to Get Psychiatric Exam." *New York Post*, January 6, 1973.

Ryan, James. "Graffiti War: City Tries to Intercept Ammo." *New York Daily News*, January 7, 1973.

_____. "Writing on the Wall for Graffiti? Yes, Say Police." *New York Daily News*, January 14, 1973.

"Fight against Subway Graffiti Progresses from Frying Pan to Fire." *New York Times*, January 26, 1973.

Kaufman, Michael T. "Boy Scouts Scrub Graffiti Off Walls of Subway Cars." *New York Times*, February 26, 1973.

Reel, William. "Graffiti Artists Erase That Greasy Kids' Stuff." *New York Daily News*, March 1, 1973.

Ranzal, Edward. "Ronan Backs Lindsay Antigraffiti Plan, Including Cleanup Duty." *New York Times*, August 29, 1972.

————— . "Officials Testify in Favor of Mayor's Graffiti Bill." *New York Times*, September 1, 1972.

"Scratch the Graffiti." *New York Times*, September 6, 1972.

"Stiff Antigraffiti Measure Passes Council Committee." *New York Times*, September 15, 1972.

Seligman, Paul. Letter to the Editor. *New York Times*, September 28, 1972.

Murray, John A. Letter to the Editor. *New York Times*, September 28, 1972.

Miele, Alfred. "Council OKs Peddling and Graffiti Bills." *New York Daily News*, October 11, 1972.

Ranzal, Edward. "Antigraffiti Bill Is One of Four Gaining Council Approval." *New York Times*, October 11, 1972.

Fischler, Stan. "Defacing New York Has Become a Real Art." *Toronto Star*, October 20, 1972.

Freeman, David. "Slop Art." *New York Times Magazine*, November 26, 1972.

Seelye, Katherine. "Underground War." *Civil Service Leader*, December 5, 1972.

Paterson, Peter R. Letter to the Editor. *New York Times*, December 6, 1972.

Harper, P. R. Letter to the Editor. *New York Times*, March 28, 1973.

Ijams, Blandinia B. "The Graffiti Nightmare." Letter to the Editor. *New York Times*, March 28, 1973.

Schumach, Murray. "At $10 Million, City Calls It a Losing Graffiti Fight." *New York Times*, March 28, 1973.

Freese, Kate M. "Camouflage Graffiti." Letter to the Editor. *New York Times*, April 2, 1973.

Baldwin, Karl R. Letter to the Editor. *New York Times*, April 4, 1973.

Pitterman, Sheldon. "To Clean the Subway Trains." Letter to the Editor. *New York Times*, April 5, 1973.

Lane, Joe. "Graffiti for the Met?" Letter to the Editor. *New York Times*, April 15, 1973.

Edmunds, Richard. "Cops Bag Nine Kids in Graffiti Grotto." *New York Daily News*, April 16, 1973.

Cohen, Patricia. "Graffiti Menacing Art." *Manhattan East*, April 17, 1973.

Ricklefs, Roger. "Co-Co 144's Underground Art Show." *Wall Street Journal*, April 26, 1973.

"The Graffiti 'Hit' Parade." *New York*, March 26, 1973

Goldstein, Richard. "This Thing Has Gotten Completely Out of Hand." *New York*, March 26, 1973.

Polster, Sandor M. "Handwriting on the Wall." *New York Post*, March 27, 1973.

Miele, Alfred. "Graffiti Makes City Scribble $10 Million Check." *New York Daily News*, March 28, 1973.

Cunliffe, Mitzi. "The Writing on the Wall." *New York Times*, July 29, 1973.

Hammond, Sally. "Some Elevating Subway Graffiti." *New York Post*, September 5, 1973.

Mason, Bryant, and Henry Lee. "Graffiti Spells Death for 'Painter,' 15." *New York Daily News*, September 8, 1973.

Van Gelder, Lindsy. "United Graffiti Artists." *New York Post*, September 8, 1973.

"Boy Spraying Graffiti Is Killed under an IND Train in Queens." *New York Times*, September 9, 1973.

Schjeldahl, Peter. "Graffiti Goes Legit—But the 'Show-off Ebullience' Remains." *New York Times*, September 16, 1973

"Underground Artists." *Newsweek*, October 1, 1973.

Bird, David. "Noise, Graffiti and Air Grate on Riders of City Subways." *New York Times*, October 11, 1973.

Clark, Alfred E. "Persistent Graffiti Anger Lindsay on Subway Tour." *New York Times*, October 11, 1973.

Torres José. "Cay 161." *New York Post*, October 13, 1973.

Kaufman, Michael T. "An Underground Graffitist Pleads from Hospital: Stop the Spraying." *New York Times*, October 18, 1973.

Slattery, William. "Graffiti Champ Scrubbed." *New York Post*, February 9, 1974.

Grossberger, Lewis. "Frank Berry Takes It Personally and He Resents the Graffiti." *New York Post*, February 15, 1974.

Mazza, Frank. "Question Plan to Use Dogs to Fight Graffiti." *New York Daily News*, July 31, 1974.

"Going to the Dogs." Editorial. *New York Times*, August 5, 1974.

"A Trial Run for Canines vs. Graffiti." *New York Post*, August 6, 1974.

Driscoll, Daniel. "The Trouble with Graffiti, It's a Catching Disease." *New York Daily News*, August 18, 1974.

Namm, Margaret W. "Art in the Subway." Letter to the Editor. *New York Times*, September 22, 1974.

"In Bronx, Trees and No Graffiti." *New York Post*, October 7, 1974.

Faso, Frank, and Paul Meskil. "Okay, Copper, Drop That Pen." *New York Daily News*, October 29, 1974.

"Policeman Facing Departmental Trial on Graffiti Charge." *New York Times*, October 29, 1974.

Hadad, Herbert. "Stationhouse Graffiti Artist Says It Wasn't One-Man Show." *New York Post*, October 29, 1974

"Policeman Tried on Graffiti Charge." *New York Times*, October 30, 1974.

"Dogs and Graffiti." *New York Times*, November 24, 1974.

Satterwhite, Sandy. "For Them Graffiti Is No Longer an Underground Movement." *New York Post*, December 24, 1974.

Ryan, James. "The Great Graffiti Plague." *New York Daily News Sunday Magazine*, May 6, 1973.

Campbell, Barbara. "Six Students' Murals Vie with Subway's Graffiti." *New York Times*, June 6, 1973.

Ryan, James. "The Mayor Charges MTA is Soft on Graffiti." *New York Daily News*, July 1, 1973.

McGovern, Michael. "Brotherhood Artists Beat Graffiti Handily." *New York Daily News*, February 21, 1974.

Carrier, James. "Docs Use Graffiti as Therapy." *New York Post*, March 1, 1974.

Sostchen, Al. "It's Grime and Punishment for Two Graffiti Artists." *New York Post*, March 7, 1974.

Tomasson, Robert E. "Graffiti Cleanups A 'Lark' For the Young." *New York Times*, April 21, 1974.

Kalech, Marc. "A Look behind Graffiti." *New York Post*, April 29, 1974.

"Scouts Turn Painters to Cover Up Graffiti." *New York Times*, May 5, 1974.

Robins, Corinne. "Faith of Graffiti." *New York Times Book Review* May 5, 1974.

Schweitzer, Seth A. "To Thwart the Graffitists." Letter to the Editor. *New York Times*, May 18, 1974.

"Press Button to Release." *New Republic*, May 25, 1974.

"They're Not Scribbling." *New York Times*, June 30, 1974.

Troyer, Stephanie F. "'Ludicrous' MTA Battle." Letter to the Editor. *New York Times*, July 30, 1974.

Burks, Edward C. "MTA to Use Dogs in Its Battle on Graffiti." *New York Times*, July 30, 1974.

O'Flaherty, Thomas. "MTA vs. Graffiti: The Wrong Battle." *New York Times*, July 31, 1974.

Ringer, Edward F. "Boy Allegedly Drawing Graffiti Killed in Chase by Subway Police." *New York Times*, January 9, 1975.

Mazza, Frank. "'Graffiti-Proof' Bus Will Roll in Test." New York *Daily News*, January 10, 1975.

"The Death of a Graffiti Painter, 14." *New York Post*, January 11, 1975.

Hudson, Edward. "Yunich Says the Transit Payroll Is Down and Will Fall Further." *New York Times*, March 19, 1975.

Schwartz, Richard. "Cops Study Graffiti in Injury Case." *New York Post*, May 21, 1975.

Kuhn, Annette. "Graffiti Nation without a Country." *Village Voice*, June 30, 1975.

Cortes, Marguerite. "Keep Graffiti Indoors." *Our Town*, July 4, 1975.

Sostchen, Al, and Rita Delfiner. "Judge Orders Two Boys to Clean School Graffiti." *New York Post*, July 10, 1975.

Haitch, Richard. "Graffiti Struggle." Letter to the Editor. *New York Times*, July 13, 1975.

Greenhouse, Steven. "Graffiti Finally Gets Welcomed Home." *Westsider*, July 24, 1975.

"Subway Graffiti Campaign Given Lower Priority." *New York Times*, August 7, 1975

Alloway, Lawrence. "Art." *Nation*, September 27, 1975.

"Some Artful Dodgers Find a Different Line." *New York Times*, March 13, 1976.

Blumenthal, Ralph. "Subways Are Rated by Experts." *New York Times*, March 18, 1976.

Hectman, Michael. "New TA Paint: Graffiti Comes Off in the Wash." *New York Post*, May 11, 1976.

Mazza, Frank. "Future for City Graffiti Artists." *New York Daily News*, May 28, 1976.

"Graffiti Removal." *New York Times*, May 28, 1976.

Duddy, James. "Subway Graffiti Artists on Right Track in Exhibit." *New York Daily News*, July 9, 1976.

Burks, Edward C. "A Subway Elongatomus? Why, It's Preposterous." *New York Times*, November 18, 1976.

Fischler, Stan, and Dave Rubenstein. "The Graffiti Gangs Are Painting the Town Red Again." *Soho Weekly News*, March 10, 1977.

"Subway Graffiti." *New York Times*, March 20, 1977.

"Paper Monsters Haunting Subways." *New York Times*, March 28, 1977.

Pienciak, Richard T. "MTA Thinks It Has a Way to Erase Tracy's $25 Subway Paintings." *New York Post*, April 5, 1977.

"Graffiti Is His Biz." *New York Daily News*, April 5, 1977.

"Art on the Lam." *Village Voice*, April 5, 1977.

Walsh, Edward R. "No Easy Mark." *New York Times*, September 18, 1977.

"Divine Graffiti." *New York Post*, November 29, 1978.

Moritz, Owen, and Richard Edmonds. "The New Subway Car: Fast, Quiet and Cool." *New York Daily News*, December 5, 1978.

Allen, Henry. "Signs of the Cryptic Scrawler." *Washington Post*, March 28, 1979.

Wagner, Robert F. Jr. "Artists Spins Subway Scheme." *New York*, April 30, 1979.

Herman, Robin. "Vandals Take Psychological Toll." *New York Times*, May 21, 1979.

Glazer, Nathan. "On Subway Graffiti in New York." *Public Interest* (Winter 1979).

Toth, Robert C. "The Writing on the Wall: Public Is Tired of Graffiti." *Los Angeles Times*, August 6, 1979.

Edmonds, Richard. "TA Dumping Toxic Wastes Into City Waters." *New York Daily News*, July 17, 1980.

_____. "$5M Paint Plan Seeks to Halt Subway Graffitists in Their Tracks." *New York Daily News*, July 21, 1980.

"First Things First," *New York Daily News*, July 22, 1980.

Stern, Carol, and Robert Stock. "Graffiti: The Plague Years." *New York Times Magazine*, October 19, 1980.

Whitcraft, Virginia. "You Get the Itch, You Gotta Paint." *New York Daily News*, October 24, 1980.

"San Francisco Students Who Cut Graffiti to Be Given Cash Awards." *New York Times*, October 2, 1977.

Dallas, Gus. "A Solution for Graffiti." *New York Daily News*, October 10, 1977.

Gooding, Richard. "The End of the Line for Graffiti." *New York Post*, October 14, 1977.

Sullivan, Patrick W. "Anti-Graffiti Chemical Called Health Hazard." *New York Post*, October 24, 1977.

"Fume Fear Halts Graffiti Work." *New York Times*, November 1, 1977.

Sullivan, Patrick W. "Graffiti Rx Washed Out for Tests." *New York Post*, November 1, 1977.

Malcolm, Andrew H. "Graffiti, 141 Giant Eyes along River Bank, Hint At Changing Japan." *New York Times*, November 10, 1977.

Dallas, Gus. "Critic-Cops Go Underground to Catch a Running Art Show." New York *Daily News*, November 20, 1977.

_____. "Graffiti Artists Have Other Blots." *New York Daily News*, November 24, 1977.

"Graffiti-Sprayer Shoots Super." *New York Post*, January 17, 1978.

Jochnowitz, George. "Save Thousands of Child-Hours Wasted on Ugly Daubings." *New York Post*, October 20, 1978.

Stivers, Cyndi. "Graffiti on Order." *New York Post*, October 17, 1978.

Wells, Jeff. "TA Cheers Judge for Attacking Graffiti." *New York Post*, October 25, 1980.

Ravitch, Richard. "Graffiti By Any Name is Vandalism." *New York Daily News*, November 11, 1980.

Goldstein, Richard. "The Fire Down Below." *Village Voice*, December 24, 1980.

Hager, Steven. "Graffiti: Is The Art World Ready For It?" *New York Daily News*, March 30, 1981.

Goldman, Ari L. "Dogs To Patrol Subway Yards." *New York Times*, September 15, 1981.

Wadler, Joyce. "Graffiti: Learn to Appreciate It." *Washington Post*, November 16, 1981.

"Who Can Do What About the Subways in New York?" *New York Times*, December 13, 1981.

Goldman, Ari L. "City to Use Pits of Barbed Wire in Graffiti War." *New York Times*, December 15, 1981.

Books

Mailer, Norman. *The Faith of Graffiti*. New York: Praeger/Alskog Publishers, 1974.

Other References

Office of Mayor John V. Lindsay. Press Release. June 27, 1972.

_____. Press release. July 31, 1972.

_____. Press release. August 28, 1972, A.M.

_____. Press release. August 28, 1972, P.M.

_____. Press release. October 4, 1972.

Boy Scouts of America. Greater New York Council. Press release. Feburary 15, 1973 (Scout Clean-up Day).

Work Plan—Graffiti Prevention Project. New York City Bureau of the Budget Report. February 26, 1973.

Cost of Graffiti to the City of New York. New York City Bureau of the Budget. March 21, 1973.

United Graffiti Artists Catalog. 1975.

New York City, MTA. *Specifications—Car Maintenance Division—Cleaning Compounds*. April 12, 1976.

NOGA Catalog. 1978.